Praise for *You're*

I have had a front seat to the life of Hallie D
adult friendships and a sister in Christ. And
of a woman—I now sit at her feet. I have read it twice already. Tears fell as I recognized
universal story of motherhood meshed literally with every one of us who walk in Christ while our own humanity trips us up. Hallie was always one of the most direct and sincere children I taught in my thirty plus years teaching. I now smile and see—it was a gift from God to teach in a straightforward and honest way. The book is a gift to women of all ages. Drink deeply. This is living water.

Jayme Stokes, mom, Nana, teacher, gardener, Jesus follower

Mothering is tough. Hallie gets that. In her book, she squarely takes on Mother Guilt—that plague of all mothers who know they are imperfect parents. That is, all of us. Even though my youngest reached adulthood thirteen years ago, I felt my own Mother Guilt melt away as I read this insightful book. Clinging to Jesus alone gives me my value as a mother, as a human, as a daughter of God. Thank you, Hallie, for blazoning this truth.

Amy Givler, MD, writer at amygivler.com and author of *Hope in the Face of Cancer: A Survival Guide for the Journey You Did Not Choose*

My mother soul did not know it had so many cracks and crevices that needed the deep shalom of God to heal some nagging doubts. What a beautiful gift to families God has given us in these pages. Thank you, Hallie, for saying yes to this assignment.

Lu Ann Butler, a seasoned mom, stepmom, and grandmother

You're Still a Good Mom is a compilation of wisdom, grace, and love that is given by the heavenly Father within motherhood. This book is an invitation by Hallie to view motherhood through the lens of our good God. Imagine having a hard motherhood day and you're sitting across the table from a friend, hot latte in hand, just letting it steamroll out. The said friend is revealing wisdom and encouragement for you to take hold of. Immediately, you feel a weight lifted and much, much lighter with every word shared—this is what the book did for me.

Alyson Owen, mom of three elementary children, writer, follower of Jesus

In the book *You're Still a Good Mom*, Hallie does a brilliant job of leading us to the truth of the gospel through motherhood. It looks our fear of failure as a mom right in the eyes and exposes the lie it is. I can personally attest to these truths she so beautiful writes. Hallie's wisdom and words have always encouraged me to keep my eyes on the Lord, abide in Him, and in turn changed my motherhood. These gospel truths have shaped who I am as a mother and how I see our good Father. Hallie has brought these truths to me in moments of darkness and doubt throughout motherhood. She has brought them in moments of celebration; she has offered encouragement in times I didn't even know to ask for it. She does this exact thing here in these pages. Hallie lovingly challenges us to fix our eyes on Jesus, not this culture, looking to Him, the One who has called and prepared our roles for us. I am so thankful Hallie will now be able to do this for so many women out there. If you're a mom, this book is a must-read.

Erica Johnson, physical therapist, mom of two

Motherhood is a sweet and challenging season that can sanctify us daily—if that's what we seek. Godly friendships have been a huge piece of morphing my motherhood into an experience that sharpens me, challenges me, and spurs me on to the Lord. Hallie has been that friend to me and through these pages, Hallie is that friend for you. I'm so thankful that her heart, humor, and wisdom has made it into your hands. What a gift to share my friend with you! Prepare to be challenged, validated, seen, and for a few belly laughs as we learn and continually remind ourselves that our motherhood isn't pass or fail—it's surrender to the One who never fails us.
Emily Jones, PhKD, LPC-S, LMTF-S, mom of 2

I have never felt so seen! Hallie takes the hard and hidden parts of motherhood straight to the feet of the King and truly shares life, abundant life, with her readers. As a mom with two kids in the depths of struggle and exhaustion, this book has reintroduced the gospel, the favor and grace of Jesus, to my tired soul.
Clara Crossland, mom of two toddlers

This isn't another book that will send you spiraling and striving to be perfect. It's also not a book that will permit you to throw your hands up and surrender to the lie that taking care of yourself is all that matters. This is a book that points you back to Jesus. It reminds you that through Him, you have been made perfect. So, you can surrender this family you've been called to steward to Him and trust His grace is sufficient for you. Your peak mothering moments aren't enough to make you perfect, but His sacrifice is. Equally important, your worst mothering moments aren't enough to exhaust His grace. Whether you're a new mom, a seasoned mom, a mom in waiting, or just a human exhausted with striving to be "enough," there's truth in these pages for you.
Laura Katzenmeyer, attorney, mom of two, special needs mom

If you are a mom, this is an absolute must-read! As a Christian mom of littles, this book was such a necessary reminder that I was never meant to be limitless. God created us with limitations to remind us that only God can truly sustain us through all the seasons of motherhood. From cover to cover, Hallie makes you feel seen and validated while also speaking truth and life into one of the hardest callings. The message in this book is life giving because it reminds us to look to the Giver of life in all things.
Lindsay Stagg, COO of Saltworks Ministries, mom of two

My children are grown and I'm now a grandmother. But even in recent years, I've sometimes raised this question in my mind. "Was I a good mom?" The Lord used this book to speak into my doubts. I wish I'd had it when I was raising my children. Thank you for writing this book, Hallie. There is a blessing in it for all moms. Yours included.
Sharon Evans, mom of three, grandmother of nine, Hallie's mom

You're Still a Good Mom unbinds the chords of haunting failure in motherhood with the truth and peace of Scripture. In an age of suffocating perfectionism, Hallie's perspective of godly motherhood highlights the beauty and need for the redemptive narrative. It is a deep breath in hope and prose.
Lindsay E. King, SLP-CCC, mom of three teens, Hallie's sister

You're *Still* a Good Mom

motherhood surrendered to the ONE who never fails

(even when you feel you have)

HALLIE DYE

Moody Publishers
CHICAGO

© 2025 by
Hallie Dye

All rights reserved. No part of this book may be reproduced in any form without permission in writing from the publisher, except in the case of brief quotations embodied in critical articles or reviews.

Unless otherwise indicated, all Scripture quotations are from the ESV® Bible (The Holy Bible, English Standard Version®), © 2001 by Crossway, a publishing ministry of Good News Publishers. Used by permission. All rights reserved. The ESV text may not be quoted in any publication made available to the public by a Creative Commons license. The ESV may not be translated in whole or in part into any other language.

Scripture quotations marked (NLT) are taken from the *Holy Bible*, New Living Translation, copyright ©1996, 2004, 2015 by Tyndale House Foundation. Used by permission of Tyndale House Publishers, Carol Stream, Illinois 60188. All rights reserved.

Some of the names and details of some stories have been changed to protect the privacy of individuals.

Edited by Ashleigh Slater
Interior design: Brandi Davis
Cover design: Kaylee Lockenour Dunn
Cover texture copyright © 2024 by natrot/Adobe Stock (248310678). All rights reserved.
Author photo: Brittiny Williams

ISBN: 978-0-8024-3461-6

Originally delivered by fleets of horse-drawn wagons, the affordable paperbacks from D. L. Moody's publishing house resourced the church and served everyday people. Now, after more than 125 years of publishing and ministry, Moody Publishers' mission remains the same—even if our delivery systems have changed a bit. For more information on other books (and resources) created from a biblical perspective, go to www.moodypublishers.com or write to:

Moody Publishers
820 N. LaSalle Boulevard
Chicago, IL 60610

1 3 5 7 9 10 8 6 4 2

Printed in the United States of America

To: Bear, Garnet, and Finn.

You three know better than anyone that I'm not a perfect mom.
There are many moments I've failed you,
and though I wish it were not so, many more to come.
But know this with certainty:
There is One who will never, ever fail you.
And He is unquestionably good.

Contents

introduction

Am I a Good Mom?

Dear Mama,

The dishwasher isn't running right. You wake to find that the three clean loads of laundry on the couch still haven't folded themselves despite being given every chance to do so. Each child needs something—now. A fight breaks out before breakfast can even be served. And you allowed yourself to stay up a little later last night since it is the only time when all are asleep, meaning no one needs you (plus, okay, you also had to know what happens in the next episode).

Only . . . one child *did* need you and was up in the night asking for water—twice. So today, you crave copious amounts of coffee. You warm said coffee for the third time by 8 a.m. only to abandon it once more to change a diaper. You remind your children to say "please" and "yes, ma'am" for what feels like the thousandth time. It seems as though you fix more snacks that end up discarded and forgotten than in mouths. Afterward, you find yourself on your knees cleaning smashed bananas off the floor while another child calls for you from the bathroom. The needs are endless, and it feels maddening. Your patience was at the end of its rope two days ago, and yet . . . life must go on. You silently wonder how you will ever make it to bedtime, much less start again tomorrow.

You're battered, exhausted, and sorely in need of a break. The problem is, if and when you do get that break, you aren't truly alone because your ever-present companion, Mom Guilt, starts up. "You aren't enough. You failed today," Mom Guilt whispers. "You must not be a good mom, or you wouldn't ache to be away from your children or lose your patience so quickly." As if you needed even more reason to despair, Mom Guilt leaves you feeling as if no amount of rest will truly refresh your soul or prepare you to go back.

The word that surfaces in your mind is *depletion*. It's the point of emotional exhaustion where not only your labor feels in vain but even your rest. Maybe it is. I've been there, too—more times than I can count. It feels like something awfully close to failure. And the worst yet most recurring question sinks in: *Am I a good mom?*

Hi, I'm Hallie. I am a wife to my high school sweetheart, Andrew, who is the funniest, most encouraging, and best man I've ever met; a mom of three wonderful children—Bear, Garnet, and Finn—and a self-proclaimed expert at mom guilt. Over the past decade, I've been a stay-at-home mom, a full-time working mom, a homeschool mom, a small-business mom, a mom of kids in elementary school, and an author/speaker/podcaster mom.

I've often questioned why in the world God has called me to so many shifts over the last ten years of my life—often feeling foolish for making every change. However, I have to wonder if it wasn't just so I could tell you this: Not one of these scenarios has ever abated my doubts and worries in this area. There's not one season or situation in there that I didn't wrestle with this soul-deep question. Many nights, I've lain in bed and asked Andrew this very thing, and I can assure you there will be many more. In the past, I've hated this cycle: replaying the highlight reel of failed expectations, wondering what I'm doing wrong, and the feeling that no matter how hard I try, I can't seem to fix it.

There are many books written from the standpoint of an expert—someone with credentials who finally moves to put their life's work on paper so that others can gain from their wisdom on a subject. Other books might be born of an experience—someone who has fought a battle or survived a season that taught them a perspective they feel compelled to share with the world. This book falls into another category entirely. I am neither an expert nor a survivor on the other side. This book was written over nearly five years *in* the battle, and every chapter has been me working out this question for myself: *Am I a good mom?*

This book is my research into Scripture and prayer because I needed to know the answer from the Author of goodness Himself. I needed to know what God's plan was for mothers. Unfortunately, there isn't a blueprint in Scripture that I can follow closely and check off as I go. That would inevitably be easier, but I also think it would entirely defeat the point.

What if we aren't failing at what we were made to do? Rather, what if we are failing at what we *thought* we were made to do?

Writing this book has helped me be almost grateful for this cycle and how it's changed the way

I see things. Now, I don't believe these feelings and emotions make us bad moms—they just make us bad gods.

What if we aren't failing at what we were made to do? Rather, what if we are failing at what we *thought* we were made to do? At what we were never intended to be? That be-all and end-all for our households? We can't find enough patience because no amount of our own deep breaths will make us a deity. We can't ever seem to get enough rest because no amount of refreshment will finally make us invincible. And we can't find enough goodness, gentleness, kindness, joy, or self-control on our own, because the truth is, no fruit can make us God.

But you and I wouldn't be the first women to try. And it didn't take sleep deprivation, chaos, or working in vain to uncover this desire either. Truth is, this is an age-old attempt that was first presented to Eve after creation. And it wasn't because she desired to be alone, to eat in peace, to close the bathroom door, or to have a clean home for longer than seven minutes. It was because she desired to be *like* God, and she found this desire even amidst absolutely perfect circumstances.

What if this realization of what we aren't could lead us to what we were designed to be and who we were always meant to reflect? Yes, even despite our failures and even *in* our failures.

Our deepest longing and deepest fear as mothers all lead back to one thing: the fear of being a bad mom. But our fear fails to answer the question: *What is a good mom?* What if we stopped asking culture and ourselves and simply asked the One who created us? What if there was a way we could surrender our mothering, along with every other part of us, to the One who never fails?

I want us to go through this journey together and ask: *What does God actually ask of us?* What if our striving really sources all the way back to the lies whispered long ago in a garden without any children yet present? Before the role of mom even existed?

Often, the feeling of failure for us as moms is found in two lies that we volley between on any given day. The first is that the work you're doing doesn't matter. You're unseen and purposeless and forgotten. The second is that your failures are so big; you're ruining your children. These lies are so opposite, yet we often hold them both on the same day.

It's time we flip this paradox and reveal it for the lies it contains. Lies that will keep us from realizing our true purpose here on earth and in our families. Lies that will keep us looking for worth in all the wrong places. Lies that, once dispelled, have the potential to be replaced with a truth so great that it could change our lives forever and, with it, the way that we mother. We must uncover this paradox and all its implications if we want to begin the journey of viewing motherhood the way God wants us to see it. We need to view *ourselves* and our worth the way He does. We have impact, but we can't save. We are important, but we are not invincible. We must admit that we do make pretty bad gods. But I know a really good One. I truly believe that if we seek Him and His will in our lives, we can be good moms not by our efforts but through surrender to His strength and because of His character.

This book is about finding our sense of worth and possessing a bold faith despite being an imperfect parent.

I want this book to serve as a tool in uprooting lies and replacing them with truth. Part of that will be digging through our beliefs and holding them up to God's Word to see how He defines a good mom. Part of it will be taking our own tendencies and holding them up to God's Word to see what being a good mom is *not*. Just as this is not a book from an expert or a survivor, this is not a parenting book. This book is about finding our sense of worth and possessing a bold faith despite being an imperfect parent. It's a book about learning how to surrender to the One who never fails—even when it feels like we have. And that, I believe, will enrich our parenting and, with it, our ability to mother the way God always intended.

With love and more honesty than you probably ever cared for,

A fellow God-fearing, truth-seeking, worth-craving mom

P.S. You're still a good mom. ♥

1

Reaching for Forbidden Fruit

Can I be real with you? Mother's Day has been a struggle for me at times. I do wake up with the full intention to soak up every minute and relish that I get to be a mom to my three kids. But I also meet this particular day with some impossible expectations. I used to think it was because I was being selfish or high-maintenance, but it's not so much that I had a checklist of things in mind like getting breakfast in bed, opening the perfect Mother's Day gift, or even receiving the most adorably written card (although, these are for sure welcome offerings). It's more about the expectations of affirmation. Mother's Day is the one day I don't have to feel like a failure.

It's the day when all motherhood failures are forgotten, and only the sacrifices and successes are remembered. However, the problem is I wake up with the mentality that I deserve all of this, that I'm owed it, and that I *need* to hear more of "Thank you" and "We see you." It's the day I await the confirmation I've been subconsciously longing for: that the work I've done and the sacrifices I've made have finally made me worthy. More than wanting to be noticed and thanked, I find myself entering this day aching to finally feel that I'm enough.

Have you felt this before? These thoughts can surface at any time of any day, but the litmus test for me that tends to indicate I've been harboring these suppressed feelings is the Mother's Day sermon. It's a good sermon every year and always something I agree with wholeheartedly. In fact, it's one I'd love on any other day, but with my impossible expectations, I cry every year. I find that if the words hold more "how to" and less "thanks for," I feel that, once again, I've failed to measure up. That even on the day when I should finally feel like enough, I still don't. I forget that even on Mother's Day, a day I confuse for *my* glory, it's still all about God.

I forget that even on Mother's Day—a day I confuse for *my* glory—it's still all about God.

I know my family loves me and is thankful for me. I know I'm appreciated. It simply boils down to this: In my most honest and ugliest confession, I want affirmation in the highest regard because this would be evidence of my being worthy. Although I feel this on many other days, I'm faced head-on with the fullness of this ugly truth on the day I think is an excuse for it. If you've ever felt this way, just know you aren't alone and that we also aren't the first.

WEEDING OUT THE LIES

Eve isn't a mother when we first meet her in the garden. She didn't have constant demands from tiny people, a cluttered or dated home, stretch marks, or days when she didn't know how she could do it again tomorrow. Her life was pretty much perfect. She had no pain, no shame, no one for comparison to tell her where she fell short, and no toil. Her work was always fruitful and ever successful. She had purpose, a clear calling, an unquestionably faithful husband, and she could walk and talk with God in this perfect home called Eden. Yet, the desire for more was possible.

In a brand-new world, where there was no question whose hand had created it, all glory went to God. It was clear that nothing was gained, achieved, or given except *through* God and *because of* God. No one could claim anything as having come from their own hands, especially worth and fulfillment. The world was His and everything in it, bringing Him glory and declaring Him alone worthy of praise. And this is the world I think we should start with because there's something about the story in the garden that boils humanity down to its core, revealing our most telling desires by removing all other distractions or possible causes for blame. No messes, no illness, no heartache, just a quiet, tranquil garden. It puts us right where we, as moms, think life would be perfect. And it was—for a while.

Next, we need to look at the serpent because this story and our story would not be the same without him. Scripture tells us in John 8:44 that "he was a murderer from the beginning" and also the father of lies. However, he is not the only guilty party. It's revealing of Satan's schemes that the serpent starts this famous conversation off with an outright lie in the form of a question. "Did God actually say, 'You shall not eat of any tree in the garden'?" (Gen. 3:1). This question's purpose wasn't to stump Eve or discover the truth. The question was masked with such obviously wrong facts to distract her from the underlying message, meant to sink in more slowly and appeal to places unseen. It was planted to take root and cause doubt by adding more to Eve's subconscious than what is really required of us by God.

Hidden beneath what likely felt like a friendly and attractive manner is the real question he wants her to consider—not aloud but in the privacy of her head, where fears and doubts have a chance to flourish. Behind the concern concealing his deception lies the actual question: *"Did God* really *ask this much of you?"* With this second meaning, Satan seeks to build camaraderie with a faux empathy that God is unreasonable—that He has asked too much and that such could even be characteristic of God. Veiled by the outright lie in the enemy's question, the underlying message begins to take root: *God is withholding from you. You could have more. Maybe He isn't good. Maybe He's not for your good.*

Eve answers with the intention of correcting the serpent, but her words also harbor misinformation. She tells him that God said, "You shall not eat of the fruit of the tree that is in the midst of the garden, neither shall you touch it, lest you die" (Gen. 3:3). The Bible, however, clearly states God's words to Adam before Eve was created in Genesis 2:16–17, and He never mentions touching the fruit—only that anyone who *ate* of it would die. This is important because *all* of God's words are so intentional, powerful, and perfectly stated that we want to be *sure* we've heard them clearly. Adding to or taking away from God's Word is not full truth.

Misunderstanding the character or goodness of God is no small thing. Who God is serves as the very foundation upon which our faith is built.

In our modern culture, we are inclined to think the whiter the lie, the less harmful it's likely to be. Unfortunately, oftentimes, the smaller the lie is, the more likely it is to go unnoticed and the less likely it is to be uprooted. But misunderstanding the character or goodness of God is no small thing. Who God is serves as the very foundation upon which our faith is built.

What's more, Eve's unintentional distortion of God's guideline is also crucial for truly grasping her perspective because *we* think of sin as occurring when she took the bite. However, based upon what she's just stated, *she* thinks of it as occurring when her fingertips first touch it. And once she does . . . and nothing happens . . . why not take a bite? So begins the slippery slope of sin.

UPROOTING THE ISSUE

The question still begs to be asked: *Why* does Eve take the bait at all? She knows the risk is death, even if she was misinformed about the specifics. Here's why I believe she did: just as it does today, sin promised Eve something she thought she could only achieve apart from God.

The serpent tells her, "You will not surely die. For God knows that when you eat of it your eyes will be opened, and you will be like God, knowing good and evil" (Gen. 3:4–5). This whole response alleviates her fear of dying, but I think the true persuader of desiring the fruit hangs on the words "*and you will be like God.*" The text says, "The woman was *convinced*. She saw that the tree was beautiful and its fruit looked delicious, and *she wanted the wisdom it would give her*" (Gen. 3:6 NLT; emphasis added).

This last verse suggests that Eve had never really even looked at the tree and its fruit before. With just one simple question, the serpent inclined her head that way for possibly the first time. Sometimes, all it takes for discontentment to take root is merely the act of looking past permissible trees covered in blessings to things we have *not* been given. This wandering of the eyes, combined with the self-righteous notion that we deserve more, is a most dangerous trap. That hidden message was beginning to appeal to Eve's desire to have worth, to be seen, to be truly recognized—on her own.

After she and Adam had partaken of the fruit and felt the weight of what they'd done, they hid. Eve fails to seek not only her true sense of worth from God but also her deliverance from shame—which He gladly frees us from. But when we believe we have to form our own worth, we can't possibly seek outside of ourselves to lay down our shame because feeling worthy and the removal of shame are tied together.

When we believe we have to form our own worth, we can't seek outside of ourselves to lay down our shame.

When God finds them in the garden and asks the weighted question of "why," Eve gives her reply: "The serpent deceived me . . . That's why I ate it" (Gen. 3:13 NLT). Oh, sis. The serpent does have fault here, because he did deceive her (as is true of his nature). However, that is not why she reached for the fruit. Eve was convinced and ate the fruit because the enemy had appealed to the desire that was already there: to be *like God*. I'm sure Eve thought fondly of God and loved Him, but in this moment, we know she desired to be like Him more than she wanted God Himself. After all, if it was more of God she wanted, she wouldn't have been looking for answers outside of His presence nor outside of the parameters He had labeled as good for her. No, Eve's desire at this moment was not to be more like God; it was to become more *godlike*.

She could have asked God about it at her first doubts. She could have taken her feelings back to Him and asked why He withheld this fruit from her. She could have asked Him for wisdom. James 1:5 says, "If you need wisdom, ask our generous God, and he will give it to you. He will not rebuke you for asking" (NLT). If it's truly wisdom she was seeking, why didn't she just ask? And why don't we? I think it's because asking implies that not only do we need help, but we need help outside of ourselves. Asking means we can't do it on our own. Asking means it comes not by our own hands. Asking God means we are not God.

The very next verse in James 1 says, "But when you ask him, be sure that your faith is in God alone. Do not waver, for a person with divided loyalty is as unsettled as a wave of the sea that is blown and tossed by the wind" (James 1:6 NLT). I think sometimes we don't ask because we have divided loyalty between God and ourselves. Asking means we will not receive the praise for the outcome because it will be due to Him. We can be sure if it's godly wisdom we are seeking, this desire will carry us closer to God Himself and His purposes, not further into our own purposes and certainly not into the very places He's told us not to go. If we ask God, and He alone must give in order for us to be filled, then we can never claim we were enough on our own.

WE ARE COVERED

The Genesis 3 scenario sounds scarily familiar, doesn't it? The truth is we *are* Eve. We take the bait all the time right from our living rooms. We have either allowed others to set such high expectations for us, or we have set impossible standards for ourselves as mothers that we feel we *must* keep laboring to finally feel like enough. And, because we function from a place of never feeling like enough as moms, we are in danger of reaching for forbidden fruit. For most of us, that will look like self-sufficiency, people-pleasing, performance, you name it. The fruit of these efforts comes in many shapes and forms. The issue with each and every one of them is that they aren't God. You see, when we're living from the anxious belief of pass or fail in every moment—of needing to build and prove our worth in our every action—we're living a life that is paying tribute to self instead of seeking to honor God.

I know what you're thinking. *Hallie, that doesn't make me like Eve! She had birds and squirrels follow her through a garden like Snow White, while I took a shower this morning for the first time in four days and then dried off with a towel that had a macaroni noodle in it!*

Eve's position was dependent on never failing. Ours is not.

I hear you, believe me, I do! I also understand the temptation here—more than you know. But let's get one thing straight. We, as believers in Christ on *this* day, have even greater perfection than Eve had. How? Salvation through the blood of Christ. Through that, we have safety. Worth. Love. All sealed and unable to be taken from us. We have been freed from past, present, and future sins, and we are seen by the Father as *righteous,* despite all the reasons we shouldn't be. Eve's position was dependent on never failing. Ours is not.

We are made perfect by the sacrifice of Jesus Christ. While we do continue to walk and stumble with Him in the journey of sanctification (becoming increasingly more like Christ), we are not dependent on our actions or efforts for salvation. The cross and *only* the cross can do that. We are quick to fault Eve for sinning *despite* perfect circumstances around her, yet we have been made perfect in His sight and *still* seek to perfect ourselves and the circumstances that surround us. If this isn't an indication of the idol within our hearts of wanting to be our own gods, I don't know what is. And the thing about idols is that they don't bring life. They promise more, but they always give less. Jesus promises abundance and then does immeasurably more.

We are enough, and we are worthy because *He's* made us so. When we labor to feel worthy and desire to be praised even though we have already been given perfect worth in Jesus Christ, we're taking the bait. We're looking past a garden of possibilities at a tree with fruit we were told not to eat. We're focusing on a tree that lacks the ability to satisfy the longing in our soul. Jesus saw our worst and still wanted us.

Salvation isn't something we are given so we can put it in our back pocket and continue down the road of becoming something of worth. Our redemption through Christ *is* our worth. It's the natural way of sanctification for us to outwardly change due to the change that's happened within us, but if we are laboring just to finally feel like we're enough, chances are it's not for the purposes of God but for our own.

The one act of Jesus Christ on the cross simultaneously crossed all of these off. Galatians 2:20 says, "My old self has been crucified with Christ. It is no longer I who live, but Christ lives in me. So I live in this earthly body by trusting in the Son of God, who loved me and gave himself for me" (NLT). If it's no longer we who live but Christ who lives in us, we now house *His* righteousness, not our own. How laughable that I'd seek to add more to the righteousness of Christ when He has already given Himself up for me. The very same God said, "This is my beloved Son, with whom I'm well pleased" (Matt. 3:17). Please hear me say, if you are now in Christ and Christ is now in you, the Father says about you, "This is my beloved daughter, with whom I am well pleased." I know, it feels too unbelievable to be true—and yet, it is. Take a deep breath and let that sink in. Let your soul rest in that for a moment.

We are enough because He is. We are worthy because He is worthy. We are seen because He saw us at our worst and loved us so much that He sought to save us. He does this at our *worst*. We weren't seen for our *best* efforts; we were seen despite our ugliest sin. We were chosen, and we were made finally and irrevocably enough and worthy to truly be with Him once more as Eve began in the garden. The idol isn't our desire to feel fulfilled and affirmed and finally enough. It's that we've *already* been deemed worthy and enough in the eyes of our Father and seek *still* to gain these elsewhere. When we try to attain worth through means of our own, we're unintentionally communicating that the grace of Christ, His sinless life and sacrifice, is either unnecessary or not enough for us.

We are enough because He is. We are worthy because He is worthy.

UNEARTHING FREEDOM

So, we begin our journey of asking if we are good moms with the realization that we aren't unfailing or unflawed. We'll never be the perfect mom; that isn't just okay—it's the unavoidable truth. It was never even expected. While it wasn't what God wanted for her, Eve didn't shock Him in the garden that day. Jesus wasn't God's plan B.

> For you know that God paid a ransom to save you from the empty life you inherited from your ancestors. And it was not paid with mere gold or silver, which lose their value. It was the precious blood of Christ, the sinless, spotless Lamb of God. God chose him as your ransom long before the world began, but now in these last days he has been revealed for your sake. (1 Peter 1:18–20 NLT)

Jesus Christ was always the rescue mission intended for us from the unconditional and unfailing love of our Father's heart. We call His love unfailing for two reasons. One is simply because He never fails. What He says He will do, He completes and fulfills totally—that includes the good work He began in you. Reason number two is that He remains steadfast even when we fail Him. The implication of this is that when He says we're redeemed, we truly are. Totally and completely. When He says He'll never leave nor forsake us no matter our failings, He really won't. Even when we fall short, He holds us, and He isn't going to let go. When we reach outside this to obtain success or worth on our own, we only reach for forbidden fruit. Our only hope, both eternally and here today, is through God alone.

When I stop to sit in this beautiful reality and allow myself to feel the freedom of this amazing truth, suddenly, I don't need praise anymore. I don't need from the world or anyone else what I have in abundance in the Lord, because I feel so loved and so seen and so precious that I want to turn and praise *Him*. Mother's Day now shifts from the day I most needed confirmation of my worth to a day of remembrance that He has redeemed every single part of me—even the way I mother. Instead of a day of dread awaiting the sentence of my trial, it's a day of rejoicing as I recall that He's already paid my debts and has declared me free with finality. To Him be the glory, forever, amen.

2

Weak Women

You know those mornings when you wake up ready? They don't happen often for most of us, but you know the ones I'm talking about. There's no dread, no fatigue threatening to throw you off course today, not even a to-do list hanging over your head—just a readiness to be joyful, patient, and the best mom ever. When you experience these mornings, you try to embrace them to their fullest. After all, it wasn't easy to get here because you haven't slept through the night in possibly years, and what you normally want is to crawl back in bed and pretend your morning class got canceled, but you never do. Mostly because you're not in college anymore and now drive a minivan stocked full of car seats and enough loose Goldfish crackers to feed a family of five. No matter. Today is different. Today, you are *determined*. Today, you *will* have joy. Today, you will be patient. Who knows? There may even be a little dancing in the kitchen (sponsored by coffee)—a real rarity for this night owl. Nothing could get you down. Not today. Not with your resolve.

Except maybe that dramatic tantrum your gifted three-year-old just performed. And the mood your five-year-old woke up in, entirely ungrateful for the amazing breakfast yours truly cooked for his truly. And the fact that neither kid will put their shoes on when asked the first, second, or even third time. And then someone talks back. And something is spilled. A mess is made. You're going to be late. And, heaven help us, the bottom falls out. How dare they.

You cooked, cleaned, prayed, served, loved, clothed, and gave your all. All for them and for their sakes, and yet your well-intended notions were not seen or appreciated. You woke up with patience and joy only to have your high hopes dashed down the drain along with your barely touched breakfast, forcing you to replace it with three cups of solace—er, coffee. You toss your hands up on your good intentions. That's it. You tried. Truce over. You ask, "Why can't we ever have a good morning around here?" So, you decide no more Mr. Nice Guy.

If our purpose is to be the mom our kids need, why does it rock our boat when they aren't the kids we need them to be?

You know, THOSE mornings.

It feels so unfair. All you wanted was to be the best mom.

When you and I get to this point, however, we must pause and ask ourselves: *What is the best mom I can be today?* While being patient and joyful and fun are great things to be, was this goal ultimately for *our kids*? Or was it for us? Was it truly so they could feel loved and seen? Or was it, maybe, so we could lay our heads down finally feeling like the successful saint of a mother we always knew we could be—if only they'd let us.

Of course, we want our children to feel loved and seen. Of

course, it's not acceptable to allow our kids to behave poorly. Of course, bad attitudes and tantrums and ungrateful spirits need to be addressed, though they will never be entirely eradicated (exhibit A: our current mood). But if our purpose is to be the mom *they* need that day, the mom that God desires for us to be, then why does it rock our boat so much when they aren't the kids we need *them* to be? When they don't have the behavior we require in order to be the mom we want to be? Why does it not just throw our emotions for a loop but, seemingly with it, our very value?

Perhaps this reactive anger bubbling to the surface isn't the effect of *actually* failing to be the mother God's called us to be. Perhaps it is that we've failed the perfect expectations we had set before us. Perhaps it is the disappointment that even with our double dose of resolve, once again, we were not able to be the perfect mom we wanted to be. And that maybe, in the ashes of our disappointment in ourselves, there's the hauntingly familiar feeling of failure.

THE FUN MOM

Several summers ago, we joined a gym. I promise it is first and foremost a gym, but I'll be honest—the pool, the splash pad, and the snack bar sold me. The week we joined, Andrew, who is fun and adventurous, came home from work and suggested we take the kids to swim before dinner. Having been at home all day, I wanted to be excited at that moment. I really did. I loved those family amenities in theory. I tried to match his enthusiasm without effort or hesitation. I wanted, for once in my life, to be the fun mom. But deep down, I had to psych myself up. Deep down, I was at war with myself to make it fun for the kids because, quite honestly, the thought of getting everyone ready and spending the evening there stressed me out.

To be fair, our kids were four, three, and one at the time. Not one of them knew how to swim, and to point out the obvious yet ridiculously hard truth: there were three of them and two of us. Having three children, we've found, is moving from man-to-man defense into zone defense. And I'm not the most athletically inclined, so zone defense next to pools of open water isn't exactly my idea of a good time. For these reasons, I internally struggled to correct my mood.

I was able to suck it up because I wanted to be the perfect mom pictured in my head so badly. We went straight to the splash pad, and the kids loved it! I mean, sure, there were some tears, and sure, we forgot the swim diaper, and sure, the concrete was scorching hot, but it really was a fun six minutes. After we exhausted the entertainment of the splash pad, they were ready to move to the pool. To their dismay, we passed by the large pool full of adolescents and arrived at the much smaller, much more deserted kiddie pool. Even so, it took constant watching to make sure someone didn't drown, everyone played nice, and the not-swim-diaper didn't explode. (Have I mentioned the glass gym on the second story overlooks the pool and the harried pool-goers?) After enough pent-up worry, I suggested we go. It was nearing dinner, and I knew we'd abruptly have five hangry wet people on our hands if we didn't head out soon.

The kids had a great time, Andrew had a great time, and honestly, I considered it a success, too. However, on the way home, I couldn't shake the inner turmoil from before. It wasn't even really about the pool—it was something much deeper the experience merely touched on.

When we were almost home, the kids were preoccupied with talking and playing in the back seat, and I finally voiced to Andrew what was troubling me, "I just want to be the fun mom who is always loving and kind." I'm an external processor and needed to say it out loud, but I also fully expected him to assure me without pause that I was indeed all those things. Following this, I would have unquestionably chucked out all his well-meaning words since he's biased and loves me to a fault. Except, much to my surprise, he didn't. Instead, what he said caught me so off guard that it will subsequently stay with me for the rest of my life.

"Do you want a God who is always fun and loving and kind?" he asked.

That made me stop. Andrew's question had me jerking my head back—the way you do when you're taken aback—as if by exposing a double chin, we can better assess the situation. It was a question I truthfully wasn't sure how to answer. I mean, those are great qualities and characteristics I *do* believe God has, but to sum Him up as such? That seemed . . . small and insufficient. Knowing that we have absolutely no say in who God is, I chose to play along and finally landed on, "Well, I want a God that is *good*." Andrew paused for a split second, almost as if he knew what I would say, and then his next words were more life-giving than anything else he could have ever told me. "Exactly," he said. "And that encompasses a lot more than just fun and loving and kind. And that's what you're giving our kids."

I love that God isn't just good but is *for* our good. I love that my mess and mistakes don't throw Him off.

As I thought about what Andrew said, and okay, cried a little as that truth seeped deep into a weary soul that had unknowingly craved those exact words, I realized something. I couldn't simply respond with an easy "yes" to his question because, while I think those qualities sound nice, I ultimately knew deep down that I wanted a God who does the hard things and pushes me to do the hard things. I love that God isn't just good but is *for* our good and works all things for our good—even the ugly mess. I love that my mess and mistakes don't throw Him off. I love that He's safe when my circumstances aren't. His plans and my story won't always be fun. They won't always *feel* loving and kind, but they are. He always works things out for our good and His purposes. And as I grow, I realize I want *that* more than I want what I want—to be the perfect fun mom.

If prompted, maybe my kids would even say they would want me to always be fun and loving and kind, but they don't understand everything before them. Maybe the recovering people pleaser in me would even feel inclined to try to be that for them (and I've done that sometimes), but it would be in vain. If I set out every day to only possess the qualities that I *think* I should have—or that my kids or other moms would have me possess—but I fail to be who they *need* and who God is calling me to be, my children will not thank me in the long run. I cannot be faithful in being a godly mother if my sights are always set on being a fun mother. It's on days like these I lose sight of holiness as I chase after happiness. Maybe the first step in becoming the mom He's calling me to be is to lay down my agenda of what I think that is.

Perhaps the leading cause of feeling like a failure in motherhood does not come from any standards God has set at all but unspoken standards set by us and the world. Often, what we define as a "good" mom is simply one who is currently liked by her kids. But just like me, my kids won't always enjoy what's truly for their good. They won't always like what they need, and by extension, they might not like me every minute of every day. My job in becoming a good mom isn't to be liked—it's to love them enough to be what they need despite what they want.

Perhaps becoming a good mom does not mean never failing, as we know this to be an impossible task on the very first night of being a mom. Maybe becoming the mom God means for us to be is simply being a woman who, though she falls short, always turns back to the One who never does, following His bidding another day, another moment, another surrender. Perhaps being and becoming faithfully who He calls us to be today is enough. Maybe faithfulness is found just as much in our humble turning back as it is in the moments we excel.

That day at the pool, my kids had a great time. They had what they needed (even the diaper held sufficient). They were protected and taken care of, experienced something new, and just got to be kids. And while I didn't get to leave feeling like the rock star mom I often aspire to be, I *was* a good mom.

THE STRONG MOM

I've started to wonder how much of our definition of a good mom comes from the world, the thought bubbles above our heads, and others' expectations—and how much of it actually comes from God. What would happen if, instead of waking with a mile-long list of what we think we need to be, we asked Him to open our eyes to what's needed and then fuel us for it? If you and I throw aside our agendas and focus on being the vessel or Spirit-filled person God created us to be, we're being good moms. When we abide in Him through His Word and prayer, we're being good moms.

Feeling a certain way does not make you a good mom. But honest, simple obedience to an incredibly good God does.

What does God need a vessel for in this season with your kids? In what ways is He asking you to be His hands and feet for Him? What does He need you to say, do, and provide? It might be fun, but it might be hard. It might be joyful, but it might be a struggle. It might very well be both in one breath. Feeling a certain way does not make you a good mom. *Doing* those things, despite how you feel, makes you a good mom. It results from honest, simple obedience to an incredibly good God. That makes you a good mom because *He* is good, and you are His vessel. Let's take this one step further.

Our society has become so obsessed with becoming strong, independent women. On the surface, this sounds great, and it even sounds true sometimes in circles of Christian women. However, this simply isn't the biblical model for us—not because we are moms or even women—but because we profess Christ as our Lord and Savior. Let's break this "strong, independent" mentality down.

Why does this description sound desirable? Because it lends itself to self-sufficiency, as we discussed in the last chapter. Now, is there anything wrong with an industrious woman who is hardworking and capable? No, there isn't—and we'll talk about her later in the book! But when we search God's Word for Scripture on strength, there is one clear thread. Consider these verses:

> God arms me with strength,
> and he makes my way perfect. (Ps. 18:32 NLT)

The LORD is my strength and my shield;
  in him my heart trusts, and I am helped;
my heart exults,
  and with my song I give thanks to him. (Ps. 28:7)

Fear not, for I am with you;
  be not dismayed, for I am your God;
I will strengthen you, I will help you,
  I will uphold you with my righteous right hand.
(Isa. 41:10)

Seek the LORD and his strength;
  seek his presence continually! (1 Chron. 16:11)

What is the common thread? Is it to look to our inner strength? Is it to gain strength from Him so we can break away and do it on our own? No, it's to look to His strength continually. It isn't just one time. It's not just in dire times—it's *all* the time. Not only does that mean our strength will only ever come through Him alone, but it also implies that none of it will be independent of Him and His ways. If we want to be good moms, we are meant to rely on Him.

The reason I was so disappointed with myself that day at the pool was twofold. One, I was bowing to expectations of what I thought a good mom should look like instead of asking my Creator how He intended this to go. Two, I was trying to meet those expectations on my own strength. I think if we could boil my motivation in that moment to its core, I have a sneaking suspicion that this is what we might find: *I have to be innately and naturally a good, nurturing mom. If I don't just want to love every moment, if I don't just want to make memories every moment, if it doesn't come naturally from within me all the time to be patient and kind and forbearing with my children's faults, what kind of a mother does that make me?*

I'll tell you. An honest one. Because that woman doesn't exist anywhere. Here's the best news yet: that isn't how the Lord wants it anyway. If He never meant for you to walk in faith on your own strength, He also never intended you to mother without His strength. Let that shame fall away. Do you feel lighter? Do you feel freer? I know I do. When I realize that His great plan for me as a person and, by extension, as a mom is to look to Him continually, seeking His face for my every need, that age-old lie that strength and patience should just come bubbling forth on its own from within me has to die.

God never intended for you to mother without His strength.

I want to wrap up this chapter with a radical notion that the apostle Paul gives us. I don't know how you picture Paul, but he was a pretty tough guy. He faced more trials and tribulations than I can ever imagine. He shared the good news even after being threatened, stoned, rejected, hated, you name it. He left all behind to do the work of the Lord. If there were ever a strong person, it would be him. Yet, this is what the Lord taught him about strength—and this is where we need to camp.

Paul tells us in 2 Corinthians that he had a thorn in his flesh. This wasn't literal, but we don't know exactly what this figurative thorn could have been. Maybe it was a physical source of pain, or perhaps fear and anxiety that plagued him despite his prayers—we don't know. Here's what we do know. He prayed three times that the Lord would remove it from his life. And this is what the Lord told him:

> But he said to me, "My grace is sufficient for you, for my power is made perfect in weakness." Therefore I will boast all the more gladly of my weaknesses, so that the power of Christ may rest upon me. For the sake of Christ, then, I am content with weaknesses, insults, hardships, persecutions, and calamities. For when I am weak, then I am strong. (2 Cor. 12:9–11)

Man, I love that passage. Read over it again. God's grace is sufficient. For everything. He never says, "Seriously? Again? You raised your voice again? You had a great day yesterday and seven hours of sleep. You couldn't be patient today on your own?" No, He says His grace is sufficient—more than enough—for you.

What's more, His power is made *perfect* in weakness. Am I the only one freaking out right now? This is *amazing* news, because I've got weakness aplenty!

Does this mean we stop wrestling with sin and failings? Absolutely not. It means we can stop being ashamed that we need God to help us wrestle it. That's what we are supposed to do. The weakness Paul speaks of here is not the sin in our lives—instead, it's the inability to slay it on our own. You see, when we can't do it on our own, when it's clear we must depend on Him for all that we need, His strength becomes evident to others—even our children. That is why Paul, whose life mission was to make the Lord's name known, was glad to boast about his weaknesses if it highlighted the Lord's strength. Let me ask you something: Have you gotten to a place where you are glad—or even willing—to boast of your weaknesses?

Mama, release the pressure of needing to be the fun mom, the strong mom, or the mom who always wakes up ready. You are so much more, because you are being and becoming the mom they need. You're relinquishing daily what you *want* to be for what they *need* you to be and, most importantly, what God's calling you to be. That's what a good mom does. And then release the pressure that you have to do it on your own. In patience, in peace, in parenting, or even in moments of joy, on our own, we aren't strong—and we aren't supposed to be. We are weak women, and that's a good thing. Because the power of Christ rests upon us. For when we are weak, *then* we are strong.

3

Tree of Life

The world of mom dating is much scarier than actual dating. This phenomenon, which we like to call "playdates," leaves little space for error. There must be an immediate connection over something, often a quality unable to be named, that makes you leave the playdate with the hope that you've made a new mom friend.

In this realm of dating, there is no definite who texts who first, and one or both moms will undoubtedly leave the other's texts on "read" for roughly twenty-four to forty-eight hours due to the very same reasons they were unable to finish sentences in person. Unlike real dating, the snack you brought and the behavior of both you and your child can make or break the potential for a second date. It can feel like a bit of a tightrope walk, but one in which you're holding two toddlers and a baby.

Because making mom friends can be so difficult, nearly every one of my friendships has been formed over needing to bear life's burdens or share life's joys with other women in the same stage of life. As I've changed with life stages, my friend group has grown.

My older friendships are always deepening, but there's something to be said about the depth of a friendship that comes during life's most significant moments—no matter how long you've known a person. Such was the case for me and my one friend. For the sake of privacy and protection, we'll call her Sam.

SAM'S STORY

I met Sam in a very strange season—for me and for her. I felt like life was either in a chaotic whirlwind or a complete standstill, depending on how you were looking at it. All I knew was that I was struggling. Andrew and I had just had our third baby, giving us three children, all three and under. It was a whirlwind for obvious reasons and yet a standstill because other than caring for children, nothing else could happen. With all three being at home with me, only one potty trained, and all being so young, it was all I could do emotionally and physically just to be a mom. When I met Sam, I was at a birthday party for my nephew, making sure my older two were safe in the jungle gym and my youngest didn't burst out inconsolably due to hunger or simply newborn overstimulation. I was exhausted, frazzled, and barely present. Yet somehow, Sam and I connected.

> **Sam was an open book—a kind, loyal, and almost childlike soul who knew confidently what she was about in a world where so few do.**

Sam had that immediate way about her. She was one of those people I met and felt like I could let my guard down and converse with ease—even over the loud chaos that was my life. She just *saw* people. We first connected because my oldest son Bear and Sam's little girl were close in age, and we just talked life. I could tell instantly Sam was an open book—a kind, loyal, and almost childlike soul who knew confidently what she was about in a world where so few do. Maybe that was always her personality. Or perhaps that's the place a person gets to when they know their days are few.

I'm not exactly sure when Sam was diagnosed with cancer. I'd initially heard a little of her story through a mutual friend, but I didn't have firsthand details. I did learn the prognosis wasn't good, though. After a few run-in visits with Sam, I felt invested. It was a type of conviction and compassion that burned within me that could only be the work of the Holy Spirit. Even though our talks had been in public places such as birthday parties or baby showers, they had never been surface-level or muted by setting or circumstance. They felt filled with the honesty and vulnerability friends shared over a quiet cup of coffee. Nearing life's end tends to do that—rob us of time, but at the very same time, gift us perspective on its preciousness.

We were at a baby shower for my sister-in-law one day when Sam told me that there were no more treatments to be offered, and I could tell she was not at peace with it. Something in her was still fighting. It all seemed surreal to me, especially since our gathering was centered upon the anticipation of a new life beginning—not one coming to a screeching halt. In the midst of the joy and excitement around us, we just sat in the grief and the unknown and talked. After that visit, my chaotic life continued without falter, hers with homeopathic treatments and pain management, and our paths didn't cross for a while—until one Sunday.

I had received word that Sam wasn't doing well. Hearing things had taken a turn for the worse put her even more on my heart and in the forefront of my mind that Sunday. My life group had recently talked about missions and our personal callings, but it wasn't until the sermon hit on things Sam and I had discussed in our conversations about Scripture that the Holy Spirit really got my attention.

I can count on one hand the number of times during a service that I was almost physically sitting on the edge of my seat because of the Holy Spirit's prompting, and this was one of them. As I listened, I felt like I needed to go to Sam. We'd talked about deep things, but my doubts were getting the better of me. *Was I completely sure that Sam was a Christian?* She had talked about God, and we'd discussed Scripture, but did she *know* Him? Those questions are nothing to gamble with, but could I be so bold as to go and ask her myself? Would that be offensive? Was I even the person to ask someone who would soon depart from this world?

As I wrestled with my comfort zone all wrapped up in self-doubt, I thought back to our life group when we'd talked about missions. This exact thought went through my head: *Would I go to her if I were a vocational missionary or on mission somewhere, and she was in the same village?* I would, without a doubt, since she would be so near, which would be my very purpose for being there—to spread the good news of Christ. Just as swiftly followed the conviction: *What am I saying? I am on a mission. She was right here, close to me, and this might be my purpose for being here in this hour.* Although still unsure and afraid, I immediately texted her to see if I could bring dinner and see her the next day.

Since I was a stay-at-home mom at this time, our wonderful babysitter (and saver of my sanity) came that Monday so that I could visit Sam's alone. The drive there was filled with moments of questioning. Away from the noise and constant needs at my house,

I was forced to consciously think about what I was doing. I wanted to see Sam either way, but I had no idea what to expect. Other than chatting with her, I didn't even really know what I would say or do—I just knew enough to believe that if the Holy Spirit had called me there, I'd better go. I was trusting that He'd also equip me with what I needed in my obedience.

When I arrived, Sam was finishing up a visit with her doctor. I sat and waited and visited with her mother-in-law until, slowly, everyone left but Sam and me. Now was my chance—I still didn't know what to do or say. But before I had any time to worry, Sam—being Sam—cut straight to the chase. She looked at me almost as soon as the last door closed before silence had time to set in.

I knew enough to believe that if the Holy Spirit called me there, I'd better go. I trusted He'd equip me in my obedience.

"Everybody wants me to go on hospice, but I just don't know if I'm ready."

Shoving down feelings of ineptitude, I thought, *Okay, Lord. This is why I've come.*

"Are you afraid?" I asked.

She thought for a minute. "Of dying?" she clarified frankly.

"Yes." I nodded, knowing this could be my last chance with Sam, and sugarcoating wouldn't help—nor would it have been something she would appreciate under any circumstances.

She thought briefly before answering with assurance, "No. Not really. I know Jesus, and I know where I'm going."

I felt immense relief and joy at her answer, but I also had questions. I was *sure* I had felt the Holy Spirit's burning prompting to get here today. Hadn't I? I had wanted to come and see her—to visit and provide any measure of comfort I could, but . . . why the urgency in my spirit? Was I missing what God wanted me to do? But before I could think any further, she spoke again.

"I'm just so afraid to leave my daughter." My heart dropped at the words. There it was—what was holding her captive, fueling her fight but draining her peace. I nodded silently, feeling the weight of her world in my mom heart. Bear, who had just turned four, was just a year younger than her daughter.

She added to the silence, "I just worked so hard to have her, and now I have to leave."

My throat threatened to close as I sat in the heartbreak with her. I was searching and trying to fathom how one could face the unimaginable. I realized she was searching for peace, just not over her own well-being, as I'd thought. I recognized her agony because that's what moms do. We think and worry and plan and pray over our kids constantly. Facing death hadn't changed that for her. It brought forth the ultimate worry: *What will my child do if I'm not here?* We sat in silence a moment longer, as there seemed to be nothing to say in such circumstances, until her words cut once again through the heavy silence.

"You're a mom. You get it," she said.

I nodded again in acknowledgment at the unbearable. It wasn't a question, yet I recognized one in her statement as a silent plea for a real answer. For peace. For anything of substance to tell her it was okay—permission to let go and know that her daughter would be okay.

Feeling unqualified is an immense understatement. *I shouldn't be here—I can't do this. I am just a mom*, I thought. I am just a mom who can barely handle the tasks of caring for my three kids. A mom who doesn't have these conversations or even leave her house. In fact, leaving the utterly mundane and entering into such obvious eternal matters was nothing short of surreal. But I was there. I should not be answering these questions or addressing these fears I knew nothing about. And yet, I did know the fear.

This is the place moms have to come to when they go out of town. Like when we board a flight and are faced with exactly how little control we actually have in the situation—of our life and thus our children's. Before having a baby, we may have fears about our own life in certain scenarios, but after the first child is here, what becomes much more paralyzing is the question: *What will they do if I'm not here?* But when the flight lands and the fears disperse, we tend to take up what measures of control we think we have once again, forgetting the whole ordeal. But having the foreknowledge that we won't be coming back changes things.

Sam and I sat in heavy silence a moment more before I swallowed past the lump in my throat and mustered up the courage to speak. "I won't pretend for a second to know what you're going through. Because I don't," I said. "But I have wrestled with this fear before. And to move forward, I've had to trust that God is still God and that God is still good even if I am not here. That He is sovereign, and He has great plans for my children with or without me."

Now, it was her turn to nod in silence. She teared up and told me how much she needed to hear that. And while she thanked *me*, I knew it was really the Holy Spirit, and I was just the lowly vessel who showed up. I was only able to do that much by having a babysitter. We visited a little longer, and eventually, it was time for me to return home and for her to rest. I promised as I left that I would be back again soon.

I went back to her house a week later and found Sam in the same

> **The words she needed to hear in her passing, I needed to hear in my living: God is God. God is good. *Even without me.***

place in her living room. But this time, she was unaware of her surroundings and being cared for in a hospital bed. I realized later that it was evidence of her surrender. Her unresponsive state *was* her response to her fear. She had trusted God enough to let go. She had physically believed that He was not only sovereign but also good. He would love and provide for her daughter. What I never got to tell her, though—what I didn't even realize then—was that the words she needed to hear in her passing, I've needed to hear in my living: God is God. God is good. *Even without me.*

SAM'S SURRENDER

Remember that relief of stepping off the plane and reentering the world—feeling like we've escaped our fears? That release of anxiety feels amazing, and yet it's hollow. It frees us to pick up right where we left off with idolizing our control. Don't get me wrong, God is clear in His Word that we shouldn't worry or be afraid, but not because *we* have power over our lives. As I mulled over Sam's life and surrender, this began to convict me.

I *do* believe what I told Sam that day. But am I living it? Her diagnosis forced her to make the choice, knowing time was limited. That's made me ask: *What if feeling like we have all the time in the world keeps us from surrendering? And what would it even look like to surrender constant control in our lives? To actively believe this and lean into this trust in our daily lives? What if we began to see the boundaries and limitations God set for us as good?*

In the past, I have tended to think of the final scene in the garden of Eden playing out a little differently than I'm certain it actually did. Although never consciously picturing it, I sort of thought of God addressing sin, doling out each consequence, and then, to seal the deal, pointing Adam and Eve toward the exit. The problem is that it would portray Him as operating on human emotions, which we know He does not, but it would also mean that leaving the garden was part of the punishment—as if they could not live in this perfect place after partaking in sin. This is not the truth of it, though. Their relocation was undoubtedly a *consequence* of sin, as the decision was propelled by the fall, but it was not a *punishment* for it.

Although one tree tends to be featured more prominently, there were actually two trees named in the garden:

> And out of the ground the Lord God made to spring up every tree that is pleasant to the sight and good for food. The tree of life was in the midst of the garden, and the tree of knowledge of good and evil. (Gen. 2:9)

The tree of life was in the midst of the garden—maybe even in the very middle, at the heart of this creation. Two things happen before Adam and Eve exit the garden. One, God clothes them with animal skins. Yes, it took sacrifice, and it would have likely been Adam and Eve's first concept of death in the garden—an act that no doubt brought forth the weight and understanding of the cost of sin. When God clothes them with these animal skins, He is also offering them physical provision by covering their shame with His grace. They would have understood God's message that they were worth the sacrifice of an innocent animal.

Two, God holds a conversation with who we understand to be Jesus and the Holy Spirit:

> Then the LORD God said, "Look, the human beings have become like us, knowing both good and evil. What if they reach out, take fruit from the tree of life, and eat it? Then they will live forever!" (Gen. 3:22 NLT)

This tree, able to provide everything they would need to survive—to provide actual eternal life—sounds good. Who wouldn't want the guarantee against death, against the pain it brings and the fear it elicits? Who wouldn't reach for the ultimate assurance that everything will be okay? This seems like the kind of thing a good Father would want for His children.

It's true that partaking of the tree's fruit would guarantee physical needs were met and would indeed bring eternal life. But what if this eternal life offered would solidify a future in the garden just as they were—frozen forever with the chasm between them and God? They would not need Him for their deliverance and, therefore, may never reach for Him out of desperation. They would remain ultimately unable to ever be in close communion with Him as they had been before. Therefore, His decision to banish them from the garden was not punishment—it was protection. The tree would offer eternal earthly life, but it was a poor replacement for the abundant love and eternal life that God offers *with* Him. It is only in His presence that there is fullness of joy (Ps. 16:11). After sin entered the scene, no matter how

Our best attempts at mothering should seek to point our children toward God but never to replace Him in their lives.

good the tree's intent, taking away the need for God would be the greatest punishment of all.

Sometimes, we as moms try to be this tree. We want to be everything for our kids. We think that's what a good mom does, right? Fulfilling every need or want and being there for our children every step of the way? On the surface, these seem like good things. Caring for needs is undoubtedly a part of mothering. Desiring good things and providing needed things are also a part of being a mom. However, we also consciously need to turn and face our humanity and realize that even our best attempts at mothering should seek to point our children toward God but never to replace Him in their lives.

We must ask ourselves: *Would we give this fruit to our kids if we could reach out and secure it to guarantee a healthy future and a life free of trouble and toil?* Because our effort to be their everything and to be entirely invincible on our own can look this way. When I stand back and behold this truth, I can't help but be immensely grateful that though I've definitely tried, I cannot fill this void for my children. If I had succeeded, I would inevitably and eventually remove all traces of the need for God from their lives.

Let's be honest, okay? Sometimes, as Christians, we can get a little bit superstitious with our prayers. We grow afraid—and even joke—that if we ask the Lord to move in our lives, He might actually do it. That if we surrender parts of our lives and ourselves, He might do something with it. He will. But behind this common joke is a real fear directly tied to a distrust of the Lord. If we truly believe that He will not sin against us because He can't sin (1 John 3:5), and we deeply believe He has good plans (Jer. 29:11) and works things for the good of those who love Him (Rom. 8:28), and we actively take Him at His Word, then we have nothing to fear. But if there's any sliver of doubt that He is all good and is completely trustworthy, we're not going to hand over the most precious things to us. We may actually be in danger of wanting to stand between Him and our children.

Our children have a good and perfect Savior, and that is not us. But how many days do we fight tooth and nail to embody their salvation anyway? And is it ultimately for their good? Or perhaps through our daily choices to protect and provide for our kids, we are failing to believe that here and now, He has good plans for our children, both with us *and* without us.

When we embrace this truth daily—or if you're like me, a hundred times a day—it will free us up to step into our roles and be the mothers He always intended us to be: women of imperfect dependence. We don't have to do it all because He is our all. We don't have to be perfect because He is sufficient. And we definitely do not need to fear our failures because He's still in the business of covering shame with His infinite grace. Not only do we not have to fill that role, but He actually never intended us to—even in a perfect world. Just as He covered Adam and Eve in the garden with the first sacrifice, He's covered us and everything we do with the perfect sacrifice.

The amazing, wonderful gift is that if it's actually not dependent on me to raise these kids on my own, and if I believe God holds everything in His hands—including our children and their futures—then I get the *honor* of partnering with Him in His work. All of a sudden, my role as a mother shifts from stressful and heavy to beautiful and freeing.

So, what beliefs do we hold in our hearts? Our answer to that question will determine whether we are living with the knowledge and trust that Sam clung to in the end. God used me for a moment of need in Sam's life, but I can't help but wonder if God asked me there that day because *I* needed to hear those words just as much. And if I needed to hear them, maybe you do, too.

4

God with Us

For eleven years, Andrew had to be at work at 7 a.m., and for eight of those years, he worked every other weekend. I realize there are much harder things in life, but this was hard for me. For a mom with two toddlers and a baby, seeing him leave every morning at 6:30 a.m. just felt like despair. That may sound dramatic to you, but that's truly the only word I know to articulate the feeling.

I can remember vividly the many mornings when he left that I cried before his car even backed out of the driveway. I *wanted* to stay home while our kids were babies, and I was incredibly grateful to be able to do just that, as I realize not everyone can. However, I think the thing that we have a hard time acknowledging is that blessing doesn't always dispel hardship. I think that's important for us to note—two things can be true at the same time. You can be in the right place, following the Lord in obedience, and it can still be hard and heavy. There's a weightiness to walking in your calling, especially certain seasons of it.

In this particular season, I felt alone. I often wondered how I could make it through the day with little sleep. The work felt constant, the needs of my kids endless, and I felt ill-equipped and unseen in it all. Unfortunately, instead of constantly inclining my heart towards the Lord, there were many days I gave into despair and longed for an escape from the mundane service of motherhood.

ESCAPING THE MUNDANE

Do you remember my friend Sam? When I went for my second visit with her, I didn't know what condition or situation I might find, so I prepared my heart for the worst. I took my mother-in-law's homemade sourdough bread and my Bible and I walked into her living room the same way I had the week before. I found Sam in the same place, only this time, her chair had been replaced with a hospice bed, and her usual chatty behavior was replaced with slumber. I had felt the Holy Spirit's prompting to get there that day, just as I'd felt previously, and I'd learned when following Him, you show up first and ask questions later. So that's what I did. I showed up and just sat with her.

I visited with her mother-in-law for a while and then read some passages from my Bible to Sam. I read her beautiful parts of Psalms and a passage about our new heavenly bodies to come. All the while, she lay still, eyes closed, with no reply. Then, I asked if I could pray for her. As expected, she didn't answer. I went ahead and prayed. But then her caregiver needed to stir her a little to take her medicine, and though I didn't expect an answer, I felt compelled to ask her something that might seem a little weird and unconventional.

I've never forgotten hearing a speaker tell a story about feeling prompted to ask someone in the airport if she could brush their hair. I couldn't even tell you today what the reason or the exact outcome was, but her willingness to do it has stuck with me. That one random step of obedience has convicted me and loomed in my mind as even more intimidating than sharing faith with a stranger. However, I knew the moment I heard it I wanted to have that kind of bold and willing faith even when it sounded crazy to others—including myself.

> **I wanted to have the kind of bold and willing faith that sounded crazy to others—including myself.**

As they tried in vain to rouse Sam enough to take her meds, I remembered what it was like for my legs to wake up after C-sections. The fluid buildup and the inability to move them made them feel restless, and I wondered if Sam felt that way but couldn't tell us. So, without much deliberation, I asked Sam if I could rub her legs. That was the only thing she nodded emphatically about that day. So, while her caretaker tended to her meds, I did just that.

While I rubbed her calves and feet and ankles, I commented on her smooth skin and painted toenails—you know, all things girl talk. All the while, she lay asleep, but I'm *positive* I glimpsed a little smile when I complimented her fresh pedicure. After a while, when I knew she was deeply dozing again, I re-covered her legs with the blanket. I read to Sam a little longer, prayed for her again, and then said what would be my final goodbye.

Driving away, I was at war with myself. I would have gone to visit Sam no matter the need or cause, but on the way home, I couldn't help but wonder why I'd felt the Holy Spirit's prompting. *Did I make a difference? Did I do everything I was supposed to do? Was it my prompting and not His that had led me there?*

All those "why" questions that I'd been holding tumbled forth at rapid speed. It wasn't that I needed a specific reason so much as that sometimes, when God calls us to things, we expect something miraculous to follow as if it's confirmation that we were in the right place. That our obedience *did* matter. At times, that validation does come. I'm embarrassed to say that I think some selfish part of me longed deeply for purpose and craved to experience the supernatural that day—that maybe somewhere in Sam's state of consciousness she might comment on something I couldn't see that would be a little part of heaven I might carry with me when I left and walked back into the ordinary.

At that moment in time, because of our children's ages and the constancy of the season, I felt guilty when I left home for any reason because that meant someone else had to step into the chaos. As I mulled all this over and realized the visit hadn't been what I expected, a little bit of shame washed over me. I remember praying, "Lord, if you wanted me to go just to rub her legs, I was glad to do it." We don't always know the needs or what function we serve, but following the prompting of the Holy Spirit and then meeting needs that might be someone else's answer to prayer *is* supernatural.

As I contemplated this, the discrepancy dawned on me with such clarity. Why was it that with Sam, I could see the importance and feel a deep sense of joy for meeting whatever physical need she had—big or small—but I felt drudgery in returning home to meet my children's needs? Why was it that I could view making *her* comfortable as an honor but begrudge one of my kid's tenth request to have his back scratched? Why was I so keen on tasting a glimpse of heaven that I'd lost sight of experiencing it bit by bit in our home as I cared for my family?

One obvious reason is novelty. Meeting Sam's needs was out of the ordinary, and serving my children was expected. Sometimes, when service feels expected, it can cease feeling like a gift to do it. Unfortunately, like other roles of service, a mom's work is often thankless.

Meeting tangible needs touches spiritual places. You are doing the Lord's work.

But here's the thing. The person standing in the gap between your kids feeling unseen, unimportant, and neglected is *you*. Let that sink in for a moment. Every time you feed them when they're hungry, get them a cup of water in the middle of the night, create a cozy environment for them to read or play or talk, make memories through a craft or family game night, stay up late after a ball game to study for a test with them, sit with them in their heartbreak and disappointment, or scratch their back or rub their aching legs with growing pains, you are doing the Lord's work. Meeting tangible needs touches spiritual places. Realizing this totally changed how I viewed the work set before me.

EXTRAORDINARY LOVE IN ORDINARY PLACES

When I told my mom about my visit with Sam, she said something I've never forgotten. She reminded me of a lesson we'd had recently at a women's gathering at church. We'd been studying the different names of God, representing the many facets of His character. We had just recently done Immanuel, which means "God with us." It's most commonly used at Christmas because Jesus came to us both fully God and fully human, dwelling among men. He was inconceivably conceived as both Creator *and* creation with us in the flesh. Though

I'd never thought of it that way, when I wondered if I'd done enough for Sam, my mom encouraged me that simply being present with her and meeting her physical needs reflected Immanuel.

That's exactly what Jesus did. We know why He came, but why did He stay? Why would Jesus have needed to be *here* in the same flesh we live in? He was born to die to pay our debt, which we could not pay. But it says a lot that He didn't just come one day and die the next. He could have redeemed us, which would have been far more than we ever deserved. Yet He came, and He stayed. He *lingered* with us. He lived. He grew. He learned. He walked. He talked. He served. He healed. He listened. He loved. He cooked breakfast. He went to weddings. He wept with friends. He wiped tears and held hands. He welcomed people into His space. He awoke and pushed through physical exhaustion to calm storms.

There was no need too big for Jesus to fill or too small for Him to notice.

Whatever was needed, He did it, often meeting needs in the most unconventional ways. He was really and truly, *physically* God with us. He remained to love us and model how we should live our lives. Meeting personal needs expresses intimate investment in others. Jesus saw and was willing to humble Himself and get in the mess. His earthly life shows us there was no need too big for Him to fill or too small for Him to notice. And as Jesus met concrete needs, He brought spiritual healing.

Not only did Jesus meet needs, but He also experienced these tangible needs right alongside us. He knew what it meant to have His needs met. We see the human work displaying the character of God through every act of Jesus, but what we don't get to see much of in

Scripture is His own mother loving Him this way into adulthood. How many times did Mary wake with baby Jesus in the night to comfort the Comforter? Or help the Helper? How many times did she cradle the God who holds it all? How often did she pour prayers over the God who hears? How many times did she feed the Bread of Life? How countless are the ways she provided for Jehovah Jireh?

It's achingly beautiful that Mary was doing the work of Immanuel for Immanuel Himself. While we will never have the experience or identical calling that Mary held, our hearts and responses can look the same. This young woman, who was still a virgin, unmarried, and sure to be scorned for the inexplicable miracle she would bear, met her calling with a supernatural willingness and faithfulness. When the angel brought her the news of her pregnancy, she innately understood the risk of what others would think, how others could turn on her, and how it would affect the rest of her life. Yet this was her response: "Behold, I am the servant of the Lord; let it be to me according to your word" (Luke 1:38).

We don't know all the work that Mary did, but we know she was faithful. We don't know our children's plans, yet the Lord does. No matter what comes, no matter what the next season holds, we can be sure none of the tasks we are doing will be lost, wasted, or in vain when we are working for the Lord. What's so miraculous—what can never be viewed as mundane—is that now that we have the Spirit dwelling *in* us, we very palpably have Immanuel. We have God with us and now *within* us—and we get the undeserved honor and privilege of showing that everywhere we go.

Isn't that what I had been wanting most in my life? To know that I matter? For my needs and efforts to be seen? To feel important enough for someone not only to see my needs but seek to fill them?

I get to be the very person to do that for my children. Acknowledging how much despair *we* can feel over these things as moms just further shows what a huge role we are filling every single day—every moment. We are often our children's comforters. We feel like home for them because, for a time, we are their earthly home. We aren't their ultimate destination, but we do get to make them feel peaceful and loved and secure, not because of us but because of the love of Jesus Christ.

CHOSEN AND APPOINTED

It is imperative that we realize our biggest calling is not motherhood. That's not our purpose and identity in Christ. We are, first and foremost, beloved servants of Christ. He is our top priority above our husbands and children, and whom we serve above all.

However, He still calls us to invest in the people He places right in front of us. The Bible is very clear that we are to make disciples and do so by loving God and loving people. Because of this great love and truth, we can also do these things with great love. People feel the love of Christ when it is up close and personal—when it is specific to their actual needs and we are willing to get in the mess with them. Taking this notion, what ministry in our lives will be greater than those whose noses we are wiping and mouths we are almost constantly feeding? To those who talk back, yet we remain? To those who make mistakes, yet we love unswervingly?

It's common and easy for me to long to step away from this messy work of motherhood. At times, it seems to stretch on before me like the sea—unpredictable, ever-moving, and never-ending. It can leave me longing for "more important" work. I can search for "more worthy" ways to spend my time. But I'm finding that it's not about what I'm doing but how I view it. What is more important work for a servant of Christ than investing in people—eternal beings—for His sake? Who am I to say that the tasks and ministry He's given me in this season are unworthy?

Maybe today it's laundry. Maybe right now, it's bathing. Maybe it's cooking another meal even when you and I feel too weary to make it through the day. Maybe it's stopping all the chores to sit and fill our children's need for quality time. Or maybe today, it's the constant discipline or the answering of seven thousand questions. Whatever it is right where you are, it is not lost work just because it's a small task. It is not ineffective work just because it's slow progress. And it's certainly not unimportant work even when it goes unnoticed. Our work as moms does not lack eternal purpose just because it happens in ordinary, earthly spaces. It's seen, and it's building a legacy doing kingdom work we cannot yet understand. But we don't have to—we just need to be the hands and feet of Jesus.

Viewing our ministry of motherhood as our *only* calling is a lie. But viewing it as unimportant or unworthy is an even more dangerous one.

Every minute of every day, we get to be the hands and feet of Christ, laying the groundwork in our children's lives in whatever He's called us to for the day. We pave the way for Him. Yes, viewing our ministry of motherhood as our *only* calling is a lie. But viewing it as unimportant or unworthy is an even more dangerous one.

It's not lost on me that the very work I often seek to escape is the work Sam longed to be able to remain and do for her daughter.

When I don't see it as the privilege that it is, I'm believing the enemy's lie that I'm not doing anything of worth, that the life I've been given isn't a precious gift, that I don't have worth or importance, and that my work amounts to nothing and matters to no one. But it does matter. It matters to my family, and ultimately, it matters to God. When I'm walking in this truth, the loneliness and feeling of being unseen falls away as I realize that I'm not forgotten in seasons of mundane, ordinary work. I've been chosen and appointed to it.

5

Lack and Limitation

I have a confession. I was imperfect before I became a mother. I know—you're in shock, but . . . it's true. The propensity to fail and then *feel* like a failure was already there before I had children. In fact, I'm still quite capable of failing in areas outside of motherhood, and my capability *may* have even grown a little since becoming a mom. The difference was that when I fell short, or I messed things up before, it mostly affected only me.

While imperfection is not unique to those called Mom, the drive to become perfect can become weightier when we enter this realm of motherhood. Though we were aware of shortcomings and flaws we had before, we now navigate through more needs, less time, and less sleep. We are absolutely going to get into failures and what to do with them, but first, I want to ask you something: *What if some of what we call "failure" actually isn't? What if some of the restrictions you feel guilt over were actually purposefully designed?*

There's a reason why the term "mom guilt" was invented. There are countless types of guilt, but mom guilt is truly unlike anything else. I sometimes wonder if it's because, in all other types of guilt I've experienced, I knew exactly why I felt guilty and likely knew what was right or wrong before I made my choice. Mom guilt, however, is entirely its own breed. It seems to have no rhyme, reason, or respect for peace, or warning for its prey. We don't necessarily know when it's coming or where it's coming from. It rears its ugly head at the most random things, and I think it's time you and I got curious about why that is.

What if what's fueling our guilt as moms is the unrealistic expectations we didn't know we held? Have never spoken out loud? Have you ever asked yourself what your expectations are as a mom? We've talked a lot about the unrealistic expectation of feeling we need to be perfect—but we need to think for a moment about what *is* realistic. One realistic expectation I need you to put at the top of your list is to expect yourself to have needs. Maybe we should take it back to the beginning. What needs did you have before you were a mom? From basic and obvious to more complex, according to your personality, take a moment to consider—and maybe even make a list—of what you specifically need.

Somehow, in the space from my water breaking to my returning home days later with a newborn, my previous needs that were deemed fine, neutral, and even *good* felt like selfishness.

Before I was a mom, I couldn't function without sleep. I also had to eat meals and have some alone time to recenter my thoughts and peace. I needed to drink water, a cup or two of coffee, and spend time with the

Lord regularly. (I know, you're scoffing at the obvious, but stick with me here.) I needed community, quality time with Andrew, and a rough routine for my day. Every once in a while, I needed space to be creative, even if it was just putting a fun outfit together. In fact, I liked getting dressed every day because it made me feel better. Occasionally, I needed to get out and take a long walk to consider decisions I was mulling over and get out of my head a little.

These were my needs, and there's nothing bad about any of them. Many didn't get met every single day, nor did some of them get met every week, but as a whole, I tried to keep these as best I could. The crazy thing was that I didn't feel guilty or wrong for any of them. Then, the strangest thing happened—I became a mom. Somehow, in the space from my water breaking in my kitchen to returning home days later with a newborn, all my previous needs that were deemed fine, neutral, and even *good* felt like selfishness.

Did you experience this? I didn't notice it at first because it was such a subtle shift compared to the vast and blatant other changes happening during that time. In moments where I did feel it creep up, I also felt the compulsion to chastise myself. *How could a good mom be struggling after a sleepless month when she has a beautiful, healthy baby? Didn't I understand the blessing I had? How could a patient mom be impatient with her toddlers, even if it was after weeks of no alone time? Wasn't I grateful? Hadn't I listened to the church ladies when they said to savor these moments because they passed quickly? Why hadn't my capacity grown to be limitless? Didn't I now exist fully and completely to be who these children needed?*

The limitations and boundaries on my person that seemed inevitable before now felt like a constant sense of failure. I can remember the hurry sickness (the internal turmoil to get through my errands or tasks as swiftly as possible) rising up if I had to go to the store without my baby or even a doctor's appointment. What was worse, even the *desire* to have my needs met made me feel like I was a terribly ungrateful mom.

We feel that, don't we? It is as if somehow becoming a mom is supposed to fulfill our every need as we limitlessly meet every one of our children's needs. Yet, every one of us has experienced this to be an impossibility. We still need sleep. We still have to eat. We still need to take trips to the store or go to work or—*gasp*—have some time with friends. No matter what we want to become for our family, we remain restricted.

The thing about mom guilt is that it's always set on exposing what we aren't. It points out constantly what we haven't done. It fixates on our scarcity. What increases this phenomenon as mothers is that we now feel like our lack is our children's lack. Because, as a mom, what we don't have, we can't give. These subconscious worries may look like this:

- If I don't have unlimited energy and I need to sleep, my kids don't get unlimited service from me.
- If I can't be ever-present because I need to work or have time with adults, my kids won't feel seen by me 24/7.
- If I don't hold a specific strength, I can't teach it.
- If I am not innately good at everything that I expect a good mom to excel at, I'm now a failure because I've fallen short of what I think is necessary.

What if I told you that what feels like famine is actually the avenue to abundance? What feels like lack is actually for our gain? And not just ours, but also our children's.

PURPOSELY PURPOSEFUL

You and I have already talked a lot about the garden of Eden. We've gone there together and explored the possibilities of how things felt and looked. We also stared at the reality of how things were. We've overturned the lie of perfect circumstances and how Adam and Eve didn't ruin God's plan by doing exactly what they knew not to do. God is so sovereign that sin didn't deter Him. Instead, it set His plan for perfect redemption into motion. That's a beautiful balm to our hearts, yet we still realize how deeply finite we are, and we don't know what to do with that reality. I want to dig a little deeper into that and, yes, take us back to that garden once again if you'll let me.

In the book of Genesis, between the timeline of creation and the fall, we have chapter 2, which seems to take the story out of order. In chapter 1, we see that the Lord has finished creation and called it very good, and then the chapter closes with the sixth day. Chapter 2 begins with God resting on the seventh day but then goes back in time to talk about the creation of man and woman. I can't tell you exactly why Genesis is structured like this, but I do know that God intended the creation of mankind to be set apart for a reason. I like to think of it as God giving us a timeline by setting the scene in chapter 1 and then zooming in to the storyline in chapter 2.

We use all kinds of action verbs when it comes to making something. Take creativity in the kitchen, for example. We *cook* dinner. We *bake* a cake. We *make* a sandwich. Each of these verbs convey that we took separate ingredients and intentionally put them together to have the finished product, yet each one communicates a different sentiment. For instance, if I were to tell you I baked a cake, what would you picture? Probably whatever simple cake flavor is your favorite. But if I were to tell you I *created* a cake, you are likely to imagine a more elaborate version. Whether in appearance or ingredients or process, I've conveyed to you with the one word choice the intentionality I put into my craft. The word *created* here implies a certain level of delight and attention. Without saying so much, I've implied my level of care. How much more so if I were a renowned chef? Such is the same for the creation of man and woman.

For some odd reason, when we hear it's a renowned chef creating a dish, we imagine just how much intentionality and care they may have used—not to mention the level of expert skill they have honed in their field. But when we read God's Word about how He formed, created, or built man and woman, we skim over it. Perhaps it lacks the novelty of other stories or perhaps we simply expect excellence out of God to the point of seeing it as commonplace. But when we don't intentionally stop to take in the beauty and wonder, we miss so much.

Our God is a God of detail and specifics. He is intentional, all-knowing, and He does nothing without purpose. The hands of God formed man and then "breathed into his nostrils the breath of life" (Gen. 2:7). The hands of God built woman into the perfect mix of complementing and yet distinctly contrasting man. As if there could be any doubt about God's heart and ability to create something special, the words here leave no room for question. The word choices remove all traces of doubt that there is any mistake or oversight. Every single part of us was purposeful. When His Scripture tells us that we are "fearfully and wonderfully made" (Ps. 139:14), we can take those words to heart. Now, with this in mind, take a look at this verse:

> And the man and his wife were both naked and were not ashamed. (Gen. 2:25)

Scripture gives no detail that isn't there for a very good reason. So why does the Bible include that little tidbit? Of course, *naked* is meant in the literal sense—unclothed—but Scripture does not explicitly state why it is mentioned. So, I like to dig deeper and ask what's implied with them being unclothed. Well, they were vulnerable with nothing to hide, and they lived in a state of being *undisguised*. While that thought alone is hard to fathom for our time in history, which loves good shapewear and oversized sweatshirts, the Bible takes it further and tells us how they felt about it. They "were not ashamed," which meant they went about openly and freely without any guilt or embarrassment over how God made them—even their lack of covering.

***Lack* is what we don't have on our own, and *limited* is the inability to do for ourselves what only our Creator can do.**

The imagery here is that they lacked, yet needed nothing, and this wasn't wrong. It was how God intended and created them to be. In a perfect world that held no sin, He created them naked, and said it was "very good" (Gen. 1:31). He created man and woman, both lacking and limited. *Lack* is what we don't have on our own and *limited* is the inability to do for ourselves what only our Creator can do.

The whole reason Eve reached for that fruit was to become more godlike and gain knowledge that wasn't intended for her. There are characteristics reserved only for God that we were never meant to have. While we are all image bearers, created in the image of the living God, we reflect His image but do not fully embody it. These very same qualities we cannot attain should move us to the reverential fear of standing in awe of Him and who He alone is.

God is who He is because of His incommunicable characteristics. His ability to be all knowing, all powerful, ever-present, and altogether good without blemish on His own are characteristics that make Him worthy of praise and glory. They, and many other qualities, are what make Him God. They're incommunicable because try as I may, I can never translate these to my life, and I wasn't intended to. These are the very things that should lead us to standing in awe and reverence for Him. It is true that in Him, we can do anything He calls us to. We can sustain and conquer and obey in His strength, and we can even clothe ourselves in Christ's righteousness because of His grace, but apart from Him, we can do nothing. On paper, we know and believe this to be true, yet how often are we functioning as though these incommunicable characteristics aren't just attainable but are expected of us? When we don't live in a way that acknowledges we were always intended to be limited and lacking apart from Him from the beginning, we actively hold expectations that we should be more godlike.

What I'm trying to say is that lacking in some regard cannot mean failure because lack and limitation existed before sin. God intentionally designed Adam and Eve that way, then stood back, looked at their state of need, and called it "very good" (Gen. 1:31). Why would He do this? Because even in a perfect world, we were designed to have needs, and ultimately, those needs should lead us to Him.

If we fast-forward through the fall in chapter 3 and we press play at verse 8, here is what we see happen. Pay extra close attention to the first thing God asks Adam and Eve and then addresses. (Note: It wasn't their action; it was their feelings and their state.)

> And they heard the sound of the LORD God walking in the garden in the cool of the day, and the man and his wife hid

> themselves from the presence of the LORD God among the trees of the garden. But the LORD God called to the man and said to him, "Where are you?" And he said, "I heard the sound of you in the garden, and I was afraid, because I was naked, and I hid myself." He said, "*Who told you that you were naked?* Have you eaten of the tree of which I commanded you not to eat?" (Gen. 3:8–11; emphasis added)

The picture painted in chapter 3 is very much one of shame. Look back on why they felt ashamed—because they were naked. That is so interesting to me because their actions indeed changed and were sinful, but their state of lack had not changed. They weren't all of a sudden naked—they had always been. But now that they had sinned—now that they had failed—they felt the depth of what they lacked and they longed to cover it. And what does God ask them first? "Who told you that you were naked?" Think about what He said and equally what He *didn't* say.

God doesn't say, "Look at your mess." He doesn't say, "Cover yourself" or "How could you?" He doesn't look at them and say, "I thought you were better." He's their Creator—He crafted and saw their state before they did. No, He doesn't heap shame. He simply asks them what made them realize they were lacking. He points out how what they feel now isn't that they're all of a sudden limited, it's because they now see that they are.

God never meant for us to reach outside of Him for anything because His design of a limited and lacking creature was intentional.

Remember, the source of their dawning realization was called the tree of the knowledge of good and evil. Adam and Eve's awareness grew when they ate its fruit and were forced to see their limitations. I do not want to gloss over the fact that they sinned because I do believe there should be a natural and healthy remorse when we sin. However, it's interesting that the shame they named first is the knowledge of everything they *weren't*. Even though they lacked covering, that was how it was supposed to be.

I once heard it said that sin can often be encompassed into anything that causes the human race not to flourish. Brilliantly stated, that's exactly what God had created man and woman to do—to thrive in His creation despite not having covering nor the ability to do all that He could do. This was His good and perfect plan for us. He never meant for us to reach outside of Him for anything or to feel the weight of the knowledge of that tree, because His design of a limited and lacking creature was intentional. In an entirely sin-free world, God intricately and purposefully formed us to live within good boundaries. He *wanted* us to have needs. He just never wanted us to feel ashamed about them.

A SHIELD FIT FOR A KING

So how do we live in a fallen world as creatures who have sinned, but who also have limitations that aren't inherently sinful? Let's take a look at King David before he was king:

> The king is not saved by his great army;
>   a warrior is not delivered by his great strength.
> The war horse is a false hope for salvation,

and by its great might it cannot rescue.
Behold, the eye of the Lord is on those who fear him,
on those who hope in his steadfast love,
that he may deliver their soul from death
and keep them alive in famine.
Our soul waits for the Lord;
he is our help and our shield. (Ps. 33:16–20)

David understood that a king's best assets and a warrior's strength would not hold him up. The absolute best the world can give is only a false salvation. It is no different for a mom. Our best, most patient, and most loving day in our own strength is not mighty enough to save us. Yet, even in famine, the Lord will sustain and bring life. He alone is our help and shield. What I love so much is that these words were penned by a man who, yes, was a powerful king and warrior. But he also had a pivotal moment as a boy when he faced a battle that he knew he could not win in his own power, not even if he were protected by the best armor the world could offer.

When David was just a boy, forgotten and misunderstood by his older brothers and father, he encountered a challenge that was insurmountable for any man. A giant named Goliath stood against the army of Israel. We know what David would grow to become, but at this point, David's capability was keeping sheep. He lacked the experience in battle, as well as the height, muscle, and stature that age and opportunity had not yet bestowed upon him. Yet what he did not lack was courage and the belief that outside of his own capacity, God was able.

David was only present to hear the taunting words of Goliath because he was delivering food to his brothers. He tells Saul the king,

"Let no man's heart fail because of [Goliath]. Your servant will go and fight with this Philistine" (1 Sam. 17:32). When Saul points out the hopelessness of the situation David faced due to everything he lacked, David told Saul of his hope in his God: "The Lord who delivered me from the paw of the lion and from the paw of the bear will deliver me from the hand of this Philistine" (1 Sam. 17:37).

Following this statement, Saul gives David his armor to put on, but the armor engulfed David. Scripture says David "tried in vain to go, for he had not tested them" (1 Sam. 17:39). This word *tested* here means proven or tried in a trial. It's because of this very reason David removes the armor that does not belong to him. This armor, though it looked official, substantial, and even necessary in the face of the current trial, had not proven unfaltering to David personally. But the Lord had.

David knew something no one else seemed to realize: his lack was God's glory.

Instead of reaching for what he didn't have, David leans on the Lord and takes up what he did have. He grabs his staff and five smooth stones in his shepherd's pouch along with his sling. This is the part that I love. If we could be spectators, not only would the size difference be so glaringly unbalanced, but Goliath the Philistine comes forth with a shield bearer in front of him, a companion to shield and aid him. Goliath is larger, more intimidating, stronger, and he's visibly not alone. Then there is David. He's just a boy—a lowly shepherd. He holds a staff and a sling with five hidden stones, and there's no shield bearer anywhere in sight. Goliath mocks and disdains David, but David's response is this: "You come to me with a sword and with a spear and with a javelin, but I come to you in the name of the LORD of hosts, the God of the armies of Israel, whom you have defied" (1 Sam. 17:45). In the eyes of the world, David has an inferior weapon, no defense, and no shield bearer. But in the eyes of David, I believe this was a pivotal moment of faith that he would often return to in remembrance often of just who his Shield was.

David would always remember how God shielded him and covered him in ways no one and nothing else could. He knew something no one else seemed to realize: his lack was God's glory. His limitation was the avenue for the Lord to do a miracle. In each season, when David would come into contact with his unavoidable lack, he would recall that the Lord was his shield. I believe he remembered this moment of deliverance because at the first stone, Goliath fell, and David, along with the entire nation of Israel, was delivered with the help of the Lord. Unlike Saul's armor, the Lord had proven faithful and trustworthy for David and would continue to do so many times over.

I have to point out that if David had been larger than Goliath or of the same height and clad in the strongest armor, if he had been trained and was renowned for military victories, I feel pretty confident we wouldn't still be remembering the story. Our lack does not make us heroes, but it should lead us to highlight the One who is.

The difference between how David handled his lack and how I have handled mine could not be more obvious. When I haven't had what I thought I needed to be a successful mom, I've stared at my lack. I've sat in defeat against mom guilt. I've tried to make my own shield or borrow one from the world because I viewed being unable as a failure. It's not. David saw every opportunity that pushed against his limitation as an opportunity to see God as his shield. Every time he encountered what required more than he could give, he fixed his eyes on his limitless God and praised Him accordingly.

I can't help but believe with every fiber of my being that we could completely eradicate mom guilt if we'd do the same.

LIFE-GIVING LIMITATIONS

Your time and energy aren't endless. Your strength and patience aren't limitless. But they aren't supposed to be. *Who told you that you were a failure?* Don't you know that the same God who covered Adam and Eve in the garden with animal skins has covered you with the blood of the Lamb? Don't you know that the same God who defended the nation of Israel that day against an undefeated giant is defending you right now at this moment? Do you think any detail about your life slips through His fingers? You were meant to have needs so that you could feel refreshed in *Him*. You were meant to have limits that make it clear He is the One sustaining you. You aren't failing because those same limitations entered motherhood with you. Even moms have limits, and that was always the plan.

> **Motherhood can be a place filled with joy when we are honest with ourselves and our families about what we need, what we can't do, and more importantly, what He can do.**

Just like Adam and Eve, you were intentionally made. Your basic human needs and every facet of your personality were purposefully given. Just like Adam and Eve, you were created with lack and limitation. And just like them, there's a good chance you've felt shame about that. But if we'll dwell on this truth, motherhood will not be a facet of our lives riddled with guilt, but a place filled to the brim with joy when we can be honest with ourselves and our families about what we need, what we can't do, and more importantly, what He *can*.

The word *lack* communicates to us that something is deficient, missing, or not enough. There are many things we have in this world that would fit such a description. However, one thing that we do not lack is access to our good and perfect Father. We're going to have limits. We have to seek Him daily to fill those gaps.

> I sought the Lord, and he answered me
> and delivered me from all my fears.
> Those who look to him are radiant,
> and their faces shall never be ashamed.
> This poor man cried, and the Lord heard him
> and saved him out of all his troubles.
> The angel of the Lord encamps
> around those who fear him, and delivers them.
>
> Oh, taste and see that the Lord is good!
> Blessed is the man who takes refuge in him!
> Oh, fear the Lord, you his saints,
> for those who fear him have no lack!
> The young lions suffer want and hunger;
> but those who seek the Lord lack no good thing.
> (Ps. 34:4–10)

When I allow this truth to permeate my thoughts and my heart, lacking no longer feels like failure. Instead, it feels life-giving. Not only have I been limited my entire life, but even in the realm of motherhood, where more needs are often met by less energy, lack isn't failure. It's design. I wasn't meant to do any part of this job on my own, so feeling that truth acutely is very good. The beautiful freedom is that apart from Him, I lack much. But in Him and through Him, I have life to the full (John 10:10). In Him alone, I lack nothing.

6

Repentance and Repair

I experienced postpartum depression after the birth of both of my boys. The tricky thing with Bear is that I didn't realize I suffered from it until I looked back in hindsight. Everything was new and hard and changing, so I just thought I was having a rough time adjusting. I held a lot of shame because I believed I wasn't appreciative enough or as strong as other moms. However, when it happened again with Finn, my last baby, I had something different to compare it to. I'd had a blissful experience with Garnet, my daughter, and I knew it didn't have to feel this way.

With Finn, I also understood what I felt likely had much to do with having three babies to tend to, one of me, and major sleep deprivation. The trouble was that seeing the issues more clearly didn't mean any of those variables could really change. When I recall that season, it feels like all I did was lose my patience and grapple in frustration for control of my life.

At times since, I've watched other moms love the season they're in and dote on their children in real life. I've also been pulled in by the misleading highlights of social media. With both, I've felt a deep sadness that I may have missed what I see them soaking up and enjoying. I want to get a redo and be the mom who knows these moments will pass, that I will sleep again, and that they won't always be newborns who never sleep or three-year-olds with wills of iron. I wish I'd known that it wasn't my job to *control* my kids but to instruct them through thoughtful and patient discipline, rewards, and consequences that fit the crime. I look back and cringe and ask the question: *Was I just this harsh, terrible mom who had zero patience and raised my voice constantly?* I look back and wish I could go back and love my children better—that I could go back and erase my failures.

Writing this book has led me to return to that season over and over. As I have, I've found myself dissecting all of the emotions, including the regret of what I did wrong and the frustration at the sin of my anger and impatience. Sometimes, everything I failed in is all that I can see.

Last night, I plummeted into these old thought patterns because I knew I had to write this chapter today. And that's when my phone did that thing where it makes a mini home video from memories of years past. Desiring to avoid and procrastinate, I watched it until I couldn't remember why I'd even opened my phone.

Some of the videos were from those very seasons where I remember myself as that angry, bitter mom. It was the strangest thing, though, because the candid, unstaged videos contained the voice of a mom who was kind, patient, and attentive. The images held evidence of a mom who researched, planned, and created crafts to do with her toddlers. I witnessed a mom with a no-makeup tired smile, a messy bun on her head, a baby she wore in her wrap, and the adventures she had with her two-year-old.

Mom failures are like the sound machine on full blast. It's time to turn it off.

There were videos of singing and sweet "good mornings," even though they probably followed many "hellos" throughout the night. These images didn't reconcile at all with the person I'd concocted in my head. Those videos were proof that the angry mom I've held on trial for so long really wasn't that angry all the time. In fact, she may not have been short-tempered even 5 percent of the time.

That's the crazy thing about failures. They are *so* loud. Mom failures are like the sound machine on full blast. They become such a part of the environment for a season that we don't realize all the other things they're masking or just how loud and pervasive they've become until it's time to turn it off, and the silence prevails. Well, it's time to turn it off.

FAILING ISN'T FAILURE

Vulnerability is not my favorite practice. It often leaves in its wake a space for me to panic late in the evening after everyone's gone to bed and wonder if I've overshared and removed any semblance of goodness from my character in others' eyes. Yet, vulnerability is imperative in the Christian life. And, even though I often worry I've said too much, real vulnerability isn't oversharing or pure confession. It is, however, opening up to others in a way that reveals our weaknesses and allows us to be in a position to be hurt. We do this to let others in so *they* may be helped and feel welcome to drop their self-protection. Like I said, it's not my favorite. So, naturally, I decided just to practice vulnerability in print here.

Most likely, you picked up this book because you've felt, to some degree, a weight of shame or guilt or regret over your state as a mom. Maybe that guilt is a specific failure that lives rent-free in your mind. Perhaps it's a growing list of failures. Maybe it's all the things you feel like you didn't do or that you missed. I wish I could hug you right now and tell you it's okay. You're reading through my examples, looking at a few of yours, and wondering if your failures are too much or too far. If perhaps they're too big ever to be redeemed. No, they're not. If you shared your deepest mom fears and failures with me over coffee, I'd look at you with tears of empathy and tell you, "Yep, you're still a good mom. You haven't changed my mind, but more importantly, you haven't changed *His*."

We can and will grow in righteousness. We can and will grow in patience, kindness, goodness, and gentleness—these are the natural fruit of abiding in the presence of our God and walking in faithfulness with His Spirit. Yes, yes, and amen. But we also have to be up-front and be real and say some moments won't reflect this. In some seasons where others' needs outweigh our ability, the day demands more energy than the night replenished, and the back talking demands more patience than we could muster, we're going to feel more prone to sin. Sometimes, we're going to fail. Those failures won't be contained to the younger years, nor even the years our children are in our home.

No matter how much we grow, we will not reach perfection. I wish I could write a book about how to avoid sin forever—it would be a bestseller! But the purpose of this book isn't to teach you how to be perfect. It's about how to exist free of shame in God's grace even though we aren't perfect.

Moving forward, let's talk about when we do fail. Let's talk about repentance and repair. Let's look at the words of King David—a man who knew a whole lot about both.

> The sacrifices of God are a broken spirit;
> a broken and contrite heart, O God, you will not despise.
> (Ps. 51:17)

These words were King David's, and as we've discussed, David had great faith. Scripture actually calls him a man after God's own heart (1 Sam. 13:14). He understood a lot about God and sought God's heart in rare and beautiful ways. He had an insightful ability to get things right, because his heart was often in the right place. However, these particular words were spoken after he'd committed adultery and murder. They were spoken after he was forced to face and acknowledge his failures.

Part of the tension we feel as moms is that sometimes we try to avoid the moments we have failed because we can't stomach seeing them fully. But we have to get real about when we cast blame, hide behind excuses, and avoid being wrong. It is the strongest evidence I can give you that we still believe moms can't be wrong. We cannot fail. It's not that we don't believe this in the sense that we aren't able to—but that we aren't allowed. So, when we feel we have failed, whether it's perceived or real, we sometimes cover. We avoid. We hide. And, when we do this, it brings with it the inability to say, "I'm sorry," because we struggle to acknowledge we're capable of wrong. The fear is we'd unravel our entire identity and worth if we did. But good moms aren't ones that never fail. They're the women who

Good moms aren't ones that never fail. They're the women who return continuously to the One who never fails.

return continuously to the One who never fails. For this very reason, a crucial part of being a good mom is acknowledging when we've failed.

David was the king. He was a good king and a good man. Born to be a shepherd in the obscurity of his father's fields, David was eventually anointed, chosen, and appointed to shepherd the nation of Israel by the Lord. After it appears that David's father tried to keep him hidden away, God used the prophet Samuel to appoint David to the place where God had always intended him to be. All in all, David was in the position of king because God assigned His people to David. Let that truth sink in for a minute. God meant for David to have this authority. God *entrusted* him with it.

> And Jesse made seven of his sons pass before Samuel. And Samuel said to Jesse, "The Lord has not chosen these." Then Samuel said to Jesse, "Are all your sons here?" And he said, "There remains yet the youngest, but behold, he is keeping the sheep." And Samuel said to Jesse, "Send and get him, for we will not sit down till he comes here." And he sent and brought him in. Now he was ruddy and had beautiful eyes and was handsome. And the Lord said, "Arise, anoint him, for this is he." (1 Sam. 16:10–12)

David most likely felt that his own father did not consider him worthy, capable, or fit to be the next king. After all, Jesse did not call him to even stand in the lineup. But God passed over seven older, taller, more physically fit, more experienced, and, in the eyes of the world, more worthy candidates. It was nonsensical to pass over these men and inconvenient to call and wait for the youngest, smallest, and least experienced boy from this tucked-away place. But the Lord wasn't looking for what the world deemed worthy or experienced. When the Lord was searching for the next king of Israel, He told Samuel the prophet, "For the LORD sees not as man sees: man looks on the outward appearance, but the LORD looks at the heart" (1 Sam. 16:7). God took this boy, who didn't even seem deserving of an invitation to the consecration or the sacrifice, and called him and had him anointed right in the midst of everyone who thought this. The Lord looked past all the reasons David shouldn't have been fit for this role and set him in a position for His purposes.

The ways we enter into motherhood—and continue in motherhood—that would deem us unfit in the eyes of the world are numerous. We bring with us biases, family patterns or generational curses, baggage, selfishness, and sometimes trauma into our role of mom. Yet, the Lord has deemed you and I fit to have our children for a reason. He does not see as man sees—He looks at the heart.

STILL APPOINTED AND ANOINTED

Now, let's look at this next part of David's story:

> Then Samuel took the horn of oil and anointed him in the midst of his brothers. And the Spirit of the LORD rushed upon David *from that day forward*. (1 Sam. 16:13; emphasis added)

David had the Spirit of the Lord upon him "from that day forward." When God led Samuel to anoint David with oil, it was a physical representation of God's Spirit resting on David. It was the outward show of God's will. Two things we've got to acknowledge here:

1. God knew all that would happen in David's lifetime far before David was ever appointed.
2. David would fail *while* he was still anointed.

Years later, when David is more secure in his position—when the new wears off, and he's neck-deep in responsibility and authority—he makes a series of moral failures. Scripture tells us it was during a time when kings would be at battle, but we see David is at home. Right off the bat, he's not where he's supposed to be. Then, David sees a beautiful woman bathing on her roof. After asking about her, a servant provides a warning disguised as information by calling to David's remembrance her husband, Uriah. David does not heed this warning and instead abuses his authority and sleeps with her. As a result, she becomes pregnant. Now, David must cover his sin, so he brings Uriah home to be with his wife. Uriah comes home but refuses to be comfortable in his home or sleep with his wife while his men are off fighting for their lives, so he sleeps at the king's door. David's committed at this point to cover his shame at all costs. So, when David learns this, he sends Uriah back into battle in a location he knows Uriah will be killed, and he was (2 Sam. 11:14–24).

> **Sin doesn't go away when we ignore it. Shame doesn't dissipate when we avoid it. That's why truth and love go hand in hand.**

Now David is in the clear, sin covered, shame ignored, and moving on—except that's not how sin works. Sin doesn't go away when we ignore it. Shame doesn't dissipate when we avoid it. This is why truth and love go hand in hand. God sends the prophet Nathan to, yes, call David out, but also to give him the chance to find freedom in repentance. At the Lord's prompting, Nathan tells David a story. The story goes like this:

> And the LORD sent Nathan to David. He came to him and said to him, "There were two men in a certain city, the one rich and the other poor. The rich man had very many flocks and herds, but the poor man had nothing but one little ewe lamb, which he had bought. And he brought it up, and it grew up with him and with his children. It used to eat of his morsel and drink from his cup and lie in his arms, and it was like a daughter to him. Now there came a traveler to the rich man, and he was unwilling to take one of his own flock or herd to prepare for the guest who had come to him, but he took the poor man's lamb and prepared it for the man who had come to him." (2 Sam. 12:1–4)

Nathan has been sent to frame this offense in a way that is far enough removed that David does not recognize himself as the rich man but instead relates to the poor man. Though it's been many years since David cared for sheep, he most likely remembers the affection and connection he had with them. He recalls knowing each by their name, seeing to each of their needs, and feeling the loss acutely when one died. He understands compassion for a man's sheep. Because of this, David doesn't feel the need to protect himself from shame and guilt when listening. He's able to look fully at the rich man's sin and react objectively. David doesn't even ask what comes next—he's immediately incensed.

After David's outburst that the man deserves to die and will pay fourfold for what he's done, Nathan drops the truth. "You are the man!" (2 Sam. 12:7). Nathan proceeds to lay out all the ways David has sinned against the Lord, even after being anointed king. Alongside all that David had done, the Lord has Nathan remind David of all *He* has done for him and the consequences that will follow because of David's choices. We could stop here and feel it is justified—and it is. I want to be clear that we cannot make light of David's sin by any means. In fact, it's how grave his failings were that we use them here today. Because of this, David's consequences were equally grave. Yet, it isn't the end of David's story, nor the full heart of the Father.

> David said to Nathan, "I have sinned against the LORD." And Nathan said to David, "The LORD has put away your sin; you shall not die." (2 Sam. 12:13)

There's much we can learn from David's words, but the first of which is that they're spoken to God. Even in his darkest sin, David honors God by speaking his words and feelings to Him instead of hiding from his failings and sitting stuck in shame. As moms and, more importantly, humans, we must do the same. When we're faced head-on with our sins and failings, we need to own, confess, and take them first and foremost to the Lord.

David also acknowledges something extremely crucial about his standing with the Lord and how the Lord sees him. There's a difference between a contrite heart and shame. What's our response when we mess up? We want to fix it. We start the next day by doing more, being better, and promising ourselves we'll never grow frustrated or lose our patience again. It isn't that we don't need to act differently. We do. But the problem is that, whatever our specific method, we tend to try to *do more* in order to fix it. If we couldn't fix our sins to begin with—if it was absolutely imperative that Jesus die for them—what makes us think we'll have the capability to fix anything on our own? No, our reconciliation with the Lord through Jesus Christ doesn't give us the power to conquer sins on our own; rather, it gives us the privilege and belonging to approach God in repentance despite them.

INCREASING OUR NEED

Even though David's sins were irreversible—he absolutely couldn't undo what he had done—he had things right in his response. God doesn't desire our sacrifices to fix what we've done. In fact, sitting in shame and punishing ourselves over our sin won't fix anything but will create further separation from God. Likewise, leaning more into our own efforts to fix our mistakes isn't the solution either.

In our shame, we often make assumptions of God and His response to us. Look back at Adam and Eve. Their response was to hide in shame because they didn't know what God would do or say. Shame tells us that we cannot possibly expose our deepest sin to anyone, much less the Lord, because it will discount us from being loved and accepted. Just like Adam and Eve, we often believe if we can hide and avoid, we can protect ourselves from rejection or abandonment or being labeled as unworthy of love. We think we're holding the evidence of why we don't deserve His mercy. And honestly, we kind of are. However, we think the story ends here. Yet, just like David's, it doesn't.

After God asks Adam and Eve what happened and who told them they were naked, they try to blame. They fault each other and the serpent, and their excuses are partially true. However, no amount of casting blame will remove the blame that's on us. It doesn't matter how poorly our kids have behaved or how much we haven't slept. It may give a *cause*, but excuses have never been a way to absolve guilt. We're still accountable for our own actions, and we feel that.

Not only does God still allow Adam and Eve to be blessed, but He also increases their need for Him.

How does God handle the sin of Adam and Eve? He curses the serpent and curses the ground, but He does not curse the man and woman. I want to be clear that God gives them serious consequences for their sin. What I find most interesting, though, is that He doesn't revoke the blessing. The Lord does not look at Eve and say, "Because of your failings, you will not have children. You are unworthy to be a mother." No, He increases the hardship of becoming a mother. He does not look at Adam and say, "You failed to lead your wife, and you didn't appreciate the work I gave you, so you will no longer have a satisfying and rewarding purpose." No, He increases the hardship in the toil. Why would He do this? Yes, it's because sin does bring consequences, but there's more here. Not only does God still allow Adam and Eve to have these blessings, He is increasing their need for Him.

What I find so beautiful is that when Eve has her first son, even after the excruciating pain of no modern medicine, no pamphlet or book explaining what to expect, and not even a midwife—her words are, "With the LORD's help, I have produced a man!" (Gen. 4:1 NLT). Her failure had taught her something. It showed her the Lord's mercy, and it showed that she could not do things on her own. She would forever know this.

FAILING WELL

Bear is a rule follower. He loves to know the expectations and then to meet them—I cannot begin to imagine where he's gotten this temperament (best read with heavy sarcasm applied). When he gets in the car after school, he's very quick to tell me if he's gotten in trouble that day or has failed to meet expectations and, therefore, had consequences. After he tells me, he always wants to know, "Are you mad?"

In this question is his desire to know where he stands with me. I always reassure him, "No, I'm not mad. But what can we do differently tomorrow?" Then we troubleshoot what happened and how he can respond next time. One day in the second grade, it seemed like he was really struggling to accept my answer that I wasn't upset with him. I looked at him in the rearview mirror and confirmed again that I wasn't mad. But then I said, "Bear, messing up does not mean failure." I'll never forget what he said. He looked at me and thoughtfully said, "Okay." That one word was the best response I could have asked for. While it's a good practice to reflect on how we can grow, the best gift I could ever give—and receive—as a mom is for my child to believe it when I say he's not a failure because he failed.

That story brings tears to my eyes every time I think about it. I can't even say it out loud without crying. It is such a foundational truth that I want all of my children to have, and it's a precious memory that the Lord has gifted me with. I imagine your heart aches full and proud when you see the evidence of your children believing you when you say you'll always love them. But I also want you to see that the only way my son could get to that belief was to fail. Before, my love was just a theory. After he failed, it's a reality.

Here's where we have to stop walking in dissonance. Do we honestly think we're better parents than God? Do we believe any measure of unconditional love we have for our children is greater than what He has for us? Do we love our children any less when they fail? Absolutely not. Do we think our nature is more forgiving than His? How is it that I, a human, think I'm capable of this response with my children but that my God views me differently when I fail?

I think it's because what we think is unforgivable is that we've failed the children God has given to us. However, David failed the people he was given to shepherd, and the Lord forgave him. God gave consequences, as there always are with sin, but He did not revoke His unwavering favor. The Lord wastes nothing. Not even our sin. Because in our transgressions, He can allow us to teach transgressors His ways. In the words of David: "Then I will teach transgressors your ways, and sinners will return to you" (Ps. 51:13). Our first repair and repentance is with the Lord because it is against Him we have sinned. Then, as moms, we must take it a step further to make that repair with our children when we've sinned against them as well. Our apologies to our children are more precious than we think.

My mom is a wise woman. She is a good mom and has said many kind and encouraging things to me. However, one of my favorite things she's said to me is, "I'm sorry." You may have grown up in a home that said I'm sorry quickly and often, or you may have never heard those words. Like my mom, when I thoughtfully and humbly speak these words to one of my kids, there's a gift inside telling my child that he or she is more important than my pride. In my ownership of my mistake, I communicate to my child that my failure was my fault, not theirs.

When I apologize, it also builds a sort of resilience in my kids for when they fail. Apologies modeled well help my kids learn how to take responsibility for their actions without being crushed under the weight. If I—someone they revere and look to for so many things—can admit I was wrong and not crumble, maybe they can, too.

Our apologies as moms help model for kids how to take responsibility for actions without being crushed under the weight of them.

Because of this very thing, Garnet learned to say "I'm sorry" of her own accord at age three. This very much feels like a mom boast—and hey, I am proud of that girl! However, she didn't learn this from me being such a kind and patient mom. She learned it because I had to say I'm sorry to her enough times that she could repeat the pattern.

Listen, I wish the Lord would give me a book to share that came from my successes, but truthfully, there aren't nearly enough of those to choose from. More importantly, I learn a lot more in the times I fail. I was *only* able to teach Bear that he's not a failure when he fails because I've fallen short, and my heavenly Father has had to teach me the same truth. Garnet learned a healthy pattern of repentance and repair because of my failings. Yet, God, in His sovereignty, not only blots out my sins with the blood of the Lamb, but He uses even my transgressions as a mom to lead others to Him. He can do the same for you.

What if our children don't need to see us do everything right? Instead, what if the imperfect creatures we're raising need to see what we do with imperfections? What if they need to see a mom who owns her mistakes and then walks in grace because it means they can, too? They need to witness us not panic or melt down and try to tear apart our worth when we fail because it helps them realize their worth won't be taken from them when they mess up. When they see us approach the throne of mercy in our time of need, may our children follow us and memorize the pathway for their time of need. What if how you approach Him boldly when you need mercy and forgiveness teaches them that His character truly is good and kind and loving even in our worst moments? And if that's how He sees you, He just might love them despite their failings, too.

Because of God's unfailing love and mercy, our failings don't make us failures. Instead, they make a way for forgiveness, repentance, and repair.

In the realm of motherhood, even your failure in front of your kids and with your kids represents the love of Jesus Christ. Because of God's unfailing love and mercy, our failings don't make us failures. Instead, they make a way for forgiveness, repentance, and repair.

Although I really wasn't the angry, ever-bitter mom that I sometimes fear that I was, by the grace of God, even the times I did fail weren't wasted. Because of His great mercy, I was able to repent and repair with my children when my impatience or overstimulation got the best of me. Somehow, in His mysterious and beautiful plan for mothers, my kids have learned and will continue to learn the same. May we remember over and over His great love and forgiveness, may we return to Him in every failing, and in this, point to His goodness for our children. You're still a good mom. Take your sins to the Lord—even those you are most ashamed to admit.

Apologize to your children. Failure doesn't define you, but God can use it to shape who you're becoming and who your children will become.

7

All Who Labor

Remember the season I previously mentioned of having three kids still so young? When Finn turned one, even though we were sleeping more, there was a deep sense of fatigue I couldn't quite put my finger on. It was a time when our culture wore busyness and exhaustion like badges of honor while Sabbath and rest were, at best, whispered ideals on podcasts and blog posts. However, the latter two were certainly not a reality in my life. My heart ached for such sentiments.

Andrew saw as much, and his greatest strength and weakness is aiming to fix my struggles. It can be both heartwarming and frustrating, depending on the day. Because he knows this, one day, he called me and said, "I know this is going to make you mad." He continued, "But why don't you just get away for a few days? Go to the beach by yourself! I know you won't, but I wish you would."

My parents have a condo about a six-hour drive from where we live, so this was entirely feasible on short notice. Only, at the same time, it was completely implausible since I was a mom of a four-year-old, a two-year-old, and a one-year-old. I didn't even feel longing at his words because of the sheer impossibility of such notions. Deep down, I believed that getting away and resting is not for moms. Andrew knew I thought this, too, and that's why he peppered his suggestion with disclaimers.

Not minutes passed before my best friend, Lindsay, who lived about three hours away at the time, texted me. She was pregnant with her first baby—a miracle we had waited, lamented, and prayed over for years. She sent a picture of a lamp for her nursery and asked what I thought. It was not a strange thing for a best friend to ask. However, what *was* strange was that this middle school science teacher was shopping during school hours.

The timing of it was all too perfect, or it may have never happened. When I called her to ask about it, I discovered she was on Mardi Gras break, and the possibility of visiting her unfolded from an out-of-reach dream to a solid plan. At four o'clock that afternoon, when Andrew got home from work, I rolled out, leaving him with all three kids for the first time ever and a plan to return in a couple of days. During my drive, my two days of freedom were kicked off by three hours of worship music, podcasts, prayer, and quietness. It was a true dream for a tired mom.

Yet, on that drive, I felt like an utter failure. Exhilarated and free, of course—the radio and time were mine for the *first* time in a very *long* time—but because of that, the feeling of failure was palpable. *What kind of mom does this?* Not only was I leaving my kids, but I was leaving my husband alone with a workload of needs and household chores—the very things I ached to escape—for two entire nights! What was worse, I was leaving of my own volition—not out of necessity! To put sprinkles on mom guilt, it was all for *me*. I give you the makings of the ultimate mom fail. I was Rapunzel volleying between going on an adventure or returning to the tower.

RESTING ISN'T WEAKNESS

I've come to believe over the course of this year that the most dangerous question we could ask as moms is, "What's the point?" We've already seen the devastation of asking this question in our work and uprooted that lie, but what we need to acknowledge is how we are inclined to do so in our rest as well.

This rejection of rest starts young. You've seen it in the lives of those who call you Mama. "Why do I have to go to bed?" "Why can't we go?" Or even the flat-out, "I don't want to nap." Not understanding the purpose of rest leads to outright refusal or, at the very least, failing to make it a priority.

The question of "What's the point?" is dangerous because when we ask it, we aren't often seeking a real answer. Rather, we're just giving our reason for not resting, posed as a question, but we hold no intention of seeking truth. And just as it is with our children, "Because I said so" often isn't enough. But do you know the difference between our asking the question and our children's asking? We make our kids rest anyway; therefore, they always reap the benefits. And when they do not obey, we see the effects very clearly. We used to joke that when Bear was a baby, if he did not nap, everyone paid the penalty. However, as moms, no one makes us rest, and yet when the effects of not resting begin to come out,

When I fail to make rest a priority in my life, everyone pays the penalty.

we wonder what is wrong with us. You want to know the honest truth about when I fail to make rest a priority in my life? Everyone pays the penalty.

As I drove along, I fought the urge to turn back and pushed away questions like, "What am I doing?" Sometimes, we talk about being the boss of our feelings without any idea what that may look like. On this trip, here's what it looked like: My feelings said don't go, but I did. Feelings of selfishness tried to crowd my view, but with every mile I drove, I rebelled.

In order to fight the guilt, I began to fall into a place where we, as moms, often land with our rest. A place where rest is justified in our eyes if it brings us back as better moms. A place that says if we can get rested, that's better for our kids, right? A place that says, "Really, it's selfless." I think there's truth to this. If we refuse our rest and needs forever, we eventually run out of gas, and who does that benefit?

A significant problem with this place of justification is that it's not the real, only, or even first reason we need rest. It's a sort of loophole for guilt that softens the blow of our humanity. This may seem like it doesn't matter, but it does. Here's why. It creates within us a sort of urgency or pressure for us in our rest. It sets expectations that we must make our rest "worth it." That if we don't rest the right way or adequately or come home tired, we've failed even in our rest. In this scenario, Mom Guilt whispers, "Not only did you take time away from your family, which is selfish, but you didn't even come back refreshed and ready to serve." And you know what? We buy it. We walk away feeling like our rest was just us sleeping on the job. Therefore, even in our rest, we encounter a sense of striving. We're making rest into work.

About an hour from my destination, Andrew called to check on me and tell me they were doing great. When he did, he said something that still makes me cry when I think about it. "I want you to just enjoy this weekend. Don't worry about anything else but just enjoying it," he told me. "If you stay up late and don't get rest, that's okay. I don't want you to come home and feel like you have to be 'on' just because you've been gone. This weekend is just for your rest. Just enjoy it."

I don't think there could have been a better salve for my battered, striving heart at that moment. He spoke it because he's wonderful, but what I didn't realize at the moment was that those words were also God's message to me. That it was okay to cease just to cease. To rest for no gain. My mom mentality perceived that taking time to rest made me a failure for leaving my post, yet my husband's words told me that even in what felt like my worst, I was accepted and loved. That was the truth my heart needed to rest in. And I'd needed to push into this feeling of failure so I could see that. This is perhaps one of the most crucial reasons for rest: to step away from the helm of the ship and see it still run because God was always steering anyway.

My trip turned out to be one of the sweetest, most memorable weekends of my life. It surprised me by somehow becoming a spiritual experience. On the way, I listened to podcasts and literally laughed and cried. I turned the radio off and prayed aloud. I relished in my freedom to do the unthinkable—whatever I felt like for two days! The weekend was magical.

I slept in, stayed up late, sat in pajamas, and talked for hours about nothing and everything with Lindsay. The usual hurry sickness seemed to melt away since I had no one else's schedule to meet.

What do we know about rest? And can moms really have it?

I sat in my college town in a familiar coffee shop and posted on my brand-new blog. I shopped alone, picked up lunch from my absolute favorite sandwich spot, and had lunch with one of the sweetest college friends I hadn't seen in a long time. I was able to see her kids and sit unhurried to talk about life for an entire naptime. And in every single moment, I felt the presence of God.

I know God is always present. I believe it even though I don't always feel it. Sometimes, I don't even try to. Sometimes, the fatigue, the constant immediate needs of others, and my own needs drown out the miracle of His presence with me. This trip, this magical weekend, was a resetting of sorts—a resetting of how I viewed rest, God, and myself. For me, it was the beginning of unraveling the question: *What do we know about rest?* And the other question looming above my head: *Can moms really have rest?*

WEARINESS IS NOT A BADGE OF HONOR

When we study the Old Testament, we find that the Sabbath was made mandatory in Jewish law. A day to cease working and see God.

> "Keep the Sabbath day holy.
>   Don't pursue your own interests on that day,
> but enjoy the Sabbath
>   and speak of it with delight as the LORD's holy day.
> Honor the Sabbath in everything you do on that day,
>   and don't follow your own desires or talk idly.
> Then the LORD will be your delight.
>   I will give you great honor

and satisfy you with the inheritance I promised to your
ancestor Jacob.
I, the LORD, have spoken!" (Isa. 58:13–14 NLT)

These words in Isaiah tell us that the Sabbath was created for us to enjoy it, delight in the Lord, and cease pursuing our usual interests. It wasn't to follow one's own desires but to rest in the Lord. Through this practice, we gather that at the heart of the commanded Sabbath, the purpose was to pull our eyes away from our tasks, shift them heavenward, and do so regularly. Even though the law was a temporary guardian for redemption, the heart of the law is still good. The reasons and the motives behind it have not changed. Look at the commands in this passage:

1. *Keep it holy.* In other words, keep it set apart. Make sure you prioritize it always.
2. *Don't pursue your own interests.* At face value, this looks like "don't do anything you like." However, this speaks to pursuing your gain through work and striving. It means remembering God above all and not yourself. Seek *Him* in your rest and not how your rest can serve you.
3. *Enjoy the Sabbath.* Yes, He commanded His people to enjoy their rest. Not just have it while you stress about doing it the right way.
4. *Speak of it with delight.* Don't hide it away in shame of what others will think of you. Your rest doesn't make you lesser because weariness is not a badge of honor.

The last two commands are ones we would skip over because not only do we have to fight mom guilt head-on when we make the decision to rest and take a trip as I did, but we don't dare let any of the moms in our community group know we did because then *they* would know we were failures and bad moms, too! We want to hide from mom shame and comments like, "Oh, I could never leave mine!" But that's not what this says to do, is it? It says to speak of your rest—and to speak with *delight*. Rest is important for our souls, and we gain freedom when we speak of it with delight. But it also shows the joy of the Lord to others when we give them permission to rest through our example. Things begin to shift when they see us refusing to let guilt and striving be our lords but instead resting in the Lord our God.

Rest was created to remember God and refresh the soul, and when we speak of it as such, it's infectious.

Rest was created to remember God and refresh the soul, and when we speak of it as such, it's infectious. Our recharging encourages others to lay down their agendas and do the same. It gives other moms permission to leave their posts too.

REST IS FOR EVERYONE

This was the Sabbath created by Jewish law, but let's travel back even further before this law was created. Before sin entered the world and demanded laws to govern humanity's wayward actions. Let's travel all the way back to the very beginning—the seventh day of this place we call earth.

> So God blessed the seventh day and made it holy, because on it God rested from all his work that he had done in creation. (Gen. 2:3)

So many questions enter our minds here. One, why would God rest? Two, why is it so important? Three, why is it set apart and holy? And four, can moms really have it, and what would that look like?

1. Why did God rest?

God did not need rest—it is true. He never sleeps, and if the heart of the Sabbath is to look to God, then it would suffice to say that God Himself does not need what He alone is the giver of. So, why does He do it here?

I don't pretend to understand the mysterious thoughts and ways of God, but as a mom, I think I get this one. God may not have needed it for Himself, but His new creations would have witnessed His rest since they had already walked the earth. In fact, after roles and purposes, it was the very first lesson God taught mankind. He taught them purposeful work was good and that their worth did not change when they rested.

So much of motherhood involves correcting, teaching, and instructing with our words, but we quickly learn that the most effective method of teaching is demonstration. I give you the world of teaching manners. I must have corrected "thank you," "please," and "yes, ma'am" a thousand times before realizing my error. I was staying so vigilant about the patient reminders, but I could *not* get them to set in for my children.

One day, I saw it. "Go get your shoes on, bud." There was nothing rude about my words or tone, nothing curt or lacking kindness, but yeah, you heard it too. No "please." My subconscious reason for not including it was not that I don't believe in manners or that I fail to employ them when necessary, but that's just it. I didn't see the nicety as *necessary* simply because I was the parent. I didn't *have* to say "please" because I was in control, and when I say "put your shoes on," they should, well . . . put their shoes on. In our dynamic, I hold the authority, so my kid should do what I say regardless of what I do, right? Only . . . which would be most effective for the things I want him to deem important? Commanding them or modeling them? And so, we could expect nothing less from our good and perfect Father.

2. Why is rest so important?

I believe modeling is an effective tactic in instructing our kids, but even so, we are not unlike our children. We need to have our questions answered. I think often when people understand the *why*, they're more likely to do the *what.*

> **Rest was not a consequence of the fall. It existed in an ideal world.**

One very simple answer to why rest is important is that we are human. I can't tell you what heaven will look like, but I do believe we will work and rest, because God set the rhythm of work and rest into place before sin entered, therefore it existed in the ideal world. Rest was not a consequence of the fall. However, on this side of heaven, if for no other reason, we need it simply because we need it. Our soul is tied to a physical body with physical limitations and physical needs. Perhaps God created us this way with the very intention to ensure we'd seek rest. If He didn't make us with physical needs, would we ever seek to depend on Him for those? Since body and soul are intertwined, physical rest can bring a spiritual impact.

3. Why is rest set apart and holy?

Multiple times throughout Scripture—both in the Old and New Testaments—we see a concept related to rest that's attached to salvation and our inheritance in Christ. It is the idea of entering His rest (Heb. 3–4). This concept is hard to sum up in one chapter, let alone one sentence, but it's essentially entering into all He's given us. We liken this idea to entering heaven one day. Heaven is the ultimate rest—not just because we're leaving behind this world, but because in heaven we will enter into His presence fully.

However, we don't have to wait until heaven to enter into His rest. We can do that through His presence while we still live in the chaos and disruption and distraction and mess we have here. And, when we do rest in Him, it's a bit of heaven. It's recalling the truth that He is working everything out, that nothing slips through His fingers, and that His peace surpasses all understanding (Phil. 4:7). It's a rest that isn't totally tangible and yet is entirely palpable.

Resting on a regular basis also reminds us heaven is coming. It reminds us of what it will feel like one day—and it's a beautiful, wonderful blessing that we get to experience even a small taste of it here on earth.

But we need Him even in our rest. The reason I was struggling to leave my family for the weekend and fighting against feelings of failure with every mile I drove was because, yes, I was physically leaving my post, but I was also not fully resting in Him. He pulled me out of myself over the course of the weekend, but the beauty of experiencing His rest is that you and I don't have to leave town to find it. We don't even have to leave our cluttered living room. We need only to return to His words and His presence to find it.

> Come to me, all who labor and are heavy laden, and I will give you rest. Take my yoke upon you, and learn from me, for I am gentle and lowly in heart, and you will find rest for your souls. For my yoke is easy, and my burden is light. (Matt. 11:28–30)

The wording in these verses seems interesting, doesn't it? It sounds as though Jesus is calling out only a group of people who labor. But we know the truth is that all people are laboring for something. It's just that not all people are working as for the Lord. This passage, however, comes after Jesus speaks of unrepentant cities—those who will miss rest by refusing to come to Him at all. In it, He's calling to those who are willing to admit they can't do their life and labor alone. Only when we take upon us His teachings, follow in His ways and examples, walk with Him, and become gentle and lowly through humility will we find this rest for our souls.

On the heaviest days and weeks of motherhood or work deadlines, we can rest in the truth that we remain in Him, and He is working all things for our good. Our souls are weary because we've been trying for so long to do it on our own. Even, yes, our rest.

4. Can moms really have rest?

Rest is available and possible if you and I are willing to seek it. Yes, it is true—we don't have to move an inch from the chaos to enter into His rest. But we do have to move our pride. I realize fully that not everyone is able to leave their posts for a weekend alone, and there are some seasons where it's impossible. However, I do want you to be honest: Do you not take that time because you truly *can't*? Or do you not even seek to because it makes you feel like a failure to leave? Or, more pointedly, do you not leave because it makes you feel like a saint to stay?

When we rest, it's a reminder that even in our roles as moms, we are partnering with Him, but the work is not dependent on us.

More often than not, we don't rest because we think we are *unable*. Not that we couldn't sit still if we needed to, but that we believe we're unable to leave our work, both in motherhood and our vocational work. I think this is *exactly* why God wants us to. This goes back to relinquishing our hold on our world by stepping away from the helm of the ship and seeing it stay afloat. When we rest, it's a reminder that even in our roles as moms, we are partnering with Him, but the work is not dependent upon us.

If we think *we* are necessary in our worlds, we pale in comparison to Jesus. If we think we have a never-ending list of needs to attend to, Jesus was inundated and indispensable. People found Him everywhere, sought His healing, reached out to grab just the hem of His clothes, and flooded His home in Capernaum. He was truly *needed*—truly in high demand, truly followed (not by one, two, or three—but by the multitudes). The more He loved, the more the number grew. The more the number grew, the more He was needed. And yet, look at this passage:

> But now even more the report about him went abroad, and great crowds gathered to hear him and to be healed of their infirmities. But he would withdraw to desolate places and pray. (Luke 5:15–16)

Jesus made it a priority to withdraw and seek desolate places to be with the Father. After stepping away from heaven to be wrapped in a limited, physical body with needs, how He must have craved to enter into that rest every chance He got. If He needed it, you and I need it too. If He made it a priority, we must as well. If He sought it and craved it, Lord, may it be also with us.

REST IS PRACTICING SURRENDER

Jesus needed, craved, and modeled rest all at the same time. He was fully man and fully God and sought communion and rest in the Father. If we want to truly reflect Jesus, it would mean we diligently pull away from the many demands in order to rest. Think about what skipping this step communicates to our children or even other moms around us. We are indeed valuable to our families and impact them as moms, but when we say, "Oh, I couldn't get away," or "I could never do that," we're saying that we are indispensable. If, as mothers, we do not set boundaries in order to be alone with God, we are unintentionally stating with our actions that we *can* keep going on our own. That we don't really need Him to sustain or refresh us.

I'll be honest. Of all the chapters of this book, I've probably wrestled with this chapter the most. And it's because I struggled to boil it down to two truths that I believe moms need to hear based on everything else we've talked about. Let's start with the two lies we believe as moms:

1. We are too important in our roles and work as moms that we can't rest.
2. We aren't valuable enough for our rest to be prioritized.

However, the truth is this:

1. While our obedience and work matter, God holds all things and holds them even when we rest. He calls us to rest so we can trust Him and know He will be faithful.
2. You and I are precious to Him. He wants us to spend time with Him just as much as He wants us to enjoy the gifts His rest will bring us.

We can't do enough to earn rest, yet He tells us to take it. That's the heart of our Father.

So, here's your homework: schedule some rest.

8

Speak Truth

I have an assignment for you. I know you likely picked this book up to escape and *not* to work, but it's small, I promise. Here's the assignment: There's a mom who is on her own for the entire week. She knows she has school assignments, projects to help with, and extracurriculars to shuttle everyone to. She has a work deadline midweek, her laundry hampers are overflowing, and her youngest has been waking in the night with an ear infection. She needs groceries and hope. She knows it's her job to keep everything in the air as she figures out how to juggle it all. She's just all-around struggling. *Your* assignment is to get out a sheet of paper or use the notes app on your phone and write what you would say to her. If you encountered this mom right now, what would *you* tell her? You really have to do it, okay? All right, go.

If you're reading this sentence, you should have something on paper or typed up, be it a list or piece of advice. What did you come up with? Did you give her practical tips or an encouraging word? Did you bullet point all the checklists you would make? I know everyone's finished assignments are going to vary tremendously, but I would be willing to bet that whatever is on yours holds a generous helping of grace and encouragement. Am I right? You know how I know? Because that's what we do—we empathize with the hardship of trying to juggle it all so well because we've walked it and are quick to speak grace to that mom.

Now, here's the catch (because you knew there'd be one). That mom you were offering advice to? That mom you felt so deeply for? She's you. *You* are the one in need of a kind word and encouragement. *You* have a lot going on, and you are juggling a lot of different things. I think the fact that we are here in this book together right now would indicate that. Your life and week may not look exactly like I described; you may not be single parenting this week, or you may be a single parent every week. Either way, I'm willing to bet you have just as much on your plate, and it's a lot to hold.

What I want you to do now is return to what you wrote. Read back through it with the new recipient in mind. How does it hit when you read it for yourself? Were you gracious? Encouraging? Understanding? Here's what I want us to see: It's amazing what we'll preach to others that we won't preach to ourselves. You can't operate as though you're the first mom in history who doesn't need grace. Yes, you're strong, and yes, you can do hard things, but all moms need grace, and that includes you.

GIVE YOURSELF SOME GRACE

I realized this tendency not to give myself grace one day so clearly. So, I have to share what I noticed with you, too.

I was getting ready to go on the trip to my friend's, which I told you about in the last chapter. Fighting my feelings of failure, I was trying to set up a smooth routine and meal plan for everyone before I left. I remember with clarity walking through the grocery store and thinking through what would be easiest for Andrew to cook and prepare. I can remember physically stopping in the middle of an aisle and realizing how I was trying to make life gracious and easy for Andrew—and why? Because I knew so well the workload and the weight I was leaving behind, and I wanted to do anything in my power to alleviate as much as I could before I left. I was peppering every decision with such grace for him, but when I was in the same situation, I felt like such a failure for not doing more.

I decided to test this theory for the book, so I put up some stories on my Instagram asking moms to play along with this same prompt and respond with advice for this mom. Immediately, they began to chime in: "Let some things go." "Have frozen waffles for dinner." "Load up in pajamas and go through the Chick-fil-A drive-through." "Take a day for yourself when you can." The overarching theme was: Give. Yourself. Some. Grace.

It is our responsibility as Christians to speak truth to our own hearts.

Some of you are having red flags go up right now. You've been conditioned to tread carefully when people begin to talk about self-love, self-care, and the like. That's not bad—you and I would actually have that in common. But we can't simply stop there, close the book, and not have this conversation because what I'm about to say is important, especially if you struggle with giving yourself grace. I am not suggesting that we find within ourselves the grace, permission, or love we need—such as the self-love culture would.

I'm telling you that it is our responsibility as Christians to speak God's truth to our own hearts. We are ever ready to do that for everyone else and totally neglect to speak the truth in love to ourselves. Consider these verses:

> O Lord, who shall sojourn in your tent?
> Who shall dwell on your holy hill?
> He who walks blamelessly and does what is right
> and speaks truth in his heart. (Ps. 15:1–2)

Sometimes the reason we're struggling so much, even after knowing the truth, is that we're refusing to speak it in our own hearts. We're on the ready when someone else is in need, but we don't have such a good track record with meditating on His Word when it comes to our own needs.

We have covered all the ways we have to surrender and depend on the Lord—and grace is no exception. We have to take our thoughts captive when we begin feeling we're entering familiar patterns. Paul wrote:

> For though we walk in the flesh, we are not waging war according to the flesh. For the weapons of our warfare are not of the flesh but have divine power to destroy strongholds. We destroy arguments and every lofty opinion raised against the knowledge of God, and take every thought captive to obey Christ. (2 Cor. 10:3–5)

This book will be no help to you if you close it and never return to God's truths about you as a mom. This is something you and I have to preach in our hearts over and over. We'll have to wrestle with our doubts and take these confessions back to the Lord, who is ready and willing to remind us once more.

This is important because how we handle everything from failures to not being enough to missing important moments will communicate to those around us what we truly believe. What are we teaching about grace to those who are watching? That it truly *is* available, abundant, and sufficient for us? Or are we continuing to live under our own thumb? I would argue that never allowing yourself the grace we all desperately need is not truly allowing anyone but yourself to be the lord of your life. Because the Lord's voice doesn't sound like that. The Lord's voice is gracious, patient, and loving. His mercies never come to an end—they are new every morning (Lam. 3:22–23). If we aren't gladly accepting that for ourselves, it's stating daily we don't believe it. I would even argue that when God truly is Lord of our lives and not just Savior, grace prevails.

When God truly is Lord of our lives and not just Savior, grace prevails.

Do you know why you were so willing to offer that mom grace and mercy in her situation? It wasn't because you knew anything about her life. She was a complete and total stranger to you. You didn't know her character, her previous track record, or her manner—none of that. But what you *did* innately know is that she is doing her best, how much she cares, and ultimately, that her worth is not riding on whether she picked up takeout or watched an extra show that week. You inherently knew and believed in your heart that she was far more than someone having one abnormal week, far more than someone needing help, and entirely loved without needing to conquer the world. You didn't even question it for a minute. Why, then, do we constantly question whether we're the first person in the history of the world whose worth and value are dependent on ourselves and our efforts, not what the Lord has deemed us?

Paul spoke these words to the Galatians, who were trying to return once more to the law of Moses even after being covered by the grace of Jesus:

> How foolish can you be? After starting your new lives in the Spirit, why are you now trying to become perfect by your own human effort? Have you experienced so much for nothing? Surely it was not in vain, was it? (Gal. 3:3–4 NLT)

Clearly, by these words, motherhood isn't the only area where we struggle with perfectionism or never feel like we're enough. For many of us, motherhood is just the perfect soil for all our fears and failures to surface as we realize the sheer impossibility of becoming perfect. Paul isn't saying not to grow in righteousness or obedience to Christ. Yes, we still need to continue growing and moving toward becoming more like Christ every day, but we will not do so by believing it depends solely on us. According to these words, our efforts to become perfect through our own means make the sacrifice and our new lives in the Spirit in vain. It makes our experiences and all we've learned in vain if we return over and over to these old ways.

SEATED IN HEAVENLY PLACES

What if instead of melting into disappointment that we had the same struggle again, we memorized these words of Paul's?

> But God, being rich in mercy, because of the great love with which he loved us, even when we were dead in our trespasses, made us alive together with Christ—by grace you have been saved—and raised us up with him and seated us with him in the heavenly places in Christ Jesus, so that in the coming ages he might show the immeasurable riches of his grace in kindness toward us in Christ Jesus. For by grace you have been saved through faith. And this is not your own doing; it is the gift of God, not a result of works, so that no one may boast. For we are his workmanship, created in Christ Jesus for good works, which God prepared beforehand, that we should walk in them. (Eph. 2:4–10)

This is the gospel. Pure, simple, unblemished. That while we were at our worst, Christ died for us. Why? Because He is so rich in mercy and because of His great love for us. And then what happened to us? He seated—not future tense, but past—us with Him in heavenly places because we are already united with Christ Jesus. Tell me something. Are you living life daily clinging to the belief that even *now* we are seated in heavenly realms and united with Christ Jesus? Because when I dwell on that, it makes a lot of things that used to feel big seem rather small and inconsequential. *That* is when the grace and the joy it brings begin to seep in. If it's by grace that I have been saved, then it is by grace that I must live.

The second part of this passage that makes me sit in awe is that He did this so He can point to us in future ages as examples of the incredible wealth of His grace. Think about the word *wealth*. For illustration's sake, let's say this wealth was monetary. I've known some pretty wealthy people, and most are that way because they are wise and careful with their money. However, though they walk with wisdom on how to invest and what they should spend, they also do not live in constant fear of never having enough. They will not make daily decisions looking over their shoulder or spiraling into feelings of failure when they need to use some of their funds again. Wisdom here is not abusing wealth.

Yet, are we living as though we have "immeasurable riches of his grace" (Eph. 2:7)? As though there were more than we could ever spend? As though the supply truly was sufficient for us? It is never something we can boast about because it is not by any means of our own that we have been saved. Yet, saved we have been, and wealthy in grace we've become. Tell me, if the future generations pointed to you, would your life bear witness to this truth? Or would it look like someone trying to coast by paycheck to paycheck on your own, all the while ensuring others around you that they have enough and will never go without?

God does not operate on human emotions. There is no shortage of His grace. It will not run out—not ever.

I hope by now you know I am not proposing that we no longer put our best efforts into caring for our families. But it's not plausible to walk in a way where we'll do this and be this all the time. It is simply not humanly possible. God knows that, or He would never have sent Jesus. Good works are the *result* of our salvation and worth, not the means of achieving it.

You know what I think holds us back so often from accepting this beautiful truth so readily again and again? We believe that eventually His good and faithful patience will wear out. Eventually, He'll lose it with us. Eventually, we'll become too much, go too far, or be too constant in need of His grace. I feel it, too—it feels so otherworldly to picture anything otherwise. What human operates this way? And yet, *it is* otherworldly. God does not operate on human emotions. There is no shortage of His grace. It will not run out—not ever. Scripture tells us:

> God's law was given so that all people could see how sinful they were. But as people sinned more and more, God's wonderful grace became more abundant. (Rom. 5:20 NLT)

God's Word is very clear in the following chapter of Romans that while His grace is abundant, that abundance does not give us permission to live without care for our actions:

> For sin will have no dominion over you, since you are not under law but under grace. (Rom. 6:14)

It is true. We can no longer be dominated by sin or live like the world. Our mothering should look very different from the world's. We do not have the same permission to live aimlessly without thought for the Lord. We can't live in sin, but we also cannot live as though it's about to catch up with us either.

The mom who willingly allows the grace she desperately needs into her life gives a great gift to her children. When her kids see the woman they hold in high esteem admit her need, suddenly, it does not seem so scary to admit their own to her and later to God. I want to be a mother who tells my children through my actions how readily available grace and love are to them—not only from me, but from the God who formed them.

We must continue to walk faithfully with the Lord, doing hard things and being willing to look different from the world's ways that surround us and seek to pull us in, but we must also live under the freedom of God's grace. There's a large difference between still struggling with sin and sin still having dominion over us. We'll always need forgiveness and confession—but we don't have to sit in the separation of shame anymore.

DON'T JUST BELIEVE IN GRACE, PRACTICE IT

What does it mean to seek the Lord *and* live under the freedom of His unending, ever-increasing grace? How you answer this question has the potential to change everything about your life.

My free-spirited, deep-feeling friend Erica will often tell me, "I head-know that, but I don't heart-know that," when she's struggling to apply something in her faith to her life. I always know what she means because I have head knowledge of a lot of things that my heart has yet to understand, too. I know without a doubt that God loves me, but I also can't fathom it. I think that's a large part of faith—it seems so wonderful that it's unfathomable. There are aspects of God that will always remain a mystery because no one can ever truly be like Him.

At the same time, as I've thought over Erica's words, I've come to the conclusion that for our hearts to learn what our heads already know, we must practice those things in faith. Not just read it, state it, and have it. To create a pattern in our lives, we need to *do* something. What's more, I believe how we view others will directly reflect how we think God views us.

In the past, it was evident in my spirit that I wasn't letting God's grace permeate my life. It was never so clear as the feelings that would wash over me after I dropped the kids at school or after everyone finally fell asleep—when I was removed from the situation and could assess it better in hindsight. My knee-jerk response was to allow myself to fall into the pit of despair and side with the voice that begs, "How could you?" If I raised my voice, lost my cool, forgot something my kids needed, didn't enjoy them the way I thought I ought to, or felt too tired to engage, the spiral began. *How could I do that? How could I say that? Forget what they needed? Miss that thing?* I would sit in shame and hide from God.

Constantly reminding myself of God's grace has changed my life.

But constantly reminding myself of God's grace has changed my life. Of course, I still have moments of doubt and feelings of failure—after all, I still fail! But I no longer sit in those. Now, when I drive home after school drop-off, I pray, "Lord, I was not the mom I wanted to be this morning. I was impatient, and I was distracted. I was missing the focus, but you are patient and kind, and I need *You* to lead me. I need You to show me how to handle that situation and how to discipline or respond. I cannot do it on my own."

The evidence of us walking in freedom is approaching the Lord when we want to hide. It's asking forgiveness again because we truly do believe His mercies are never-ending. It's approaching His throne of grace, not when we feel at our best, but in our worst moments—in our times of need. It's approaching His throne not timidly as one who is unsure of His reaction but boldly, with the assurance of what Scripture has told us.

> Since then we have a great high priest who has passed through the heavens, Jesus, the Son of God, let us hold fast our confession. For we do not have a high priest who is unable to sympathize with our weaknesses, but one who in every respect has been

> tempted as we are, yet without sin. Let us then with confidence draw near to the throne of grace, that we may receive mercy and find grace to help in time of need. (Heb. 4:14–16)

We don't have an unfeeling, short-tempered High Priest. He sympathizes with our weaknesses so we can hold fast to our confession. We can draw near to Him in confidence—again, not at our best—to receive mercy and to find grace in our time of need. I think if we're being honest with ourselves, sometimes what can be hard to picture is that we don't always parent this way. We have walked through childhood yet often forget. We have had nightmares, yet we can be impatient when our children's bad dreams wreak havoc on our sleep. We have been poor listeners and slow obeyers, yet we can go from zero to ninety when we see the same in our children. Unlike us, Jesus experienced it all but without sin. Yet, this does not make Him unsympathetic.

Trust, faith, and grace must align to become action.

If we feel grace needs to be deserved before we give it to others, there will be scenarios and situations in life where grace is never given. Sometimes, people never change, never apologize, never see their faults. Just like us.

Imagine your child has done something they are ashamed of. It's been eating at them all day, and they are only five, so they don't even have words for what they're feeling. All they know is that somewhere in their hearts, they feel unworthy to tell you what has happened or what they've done, because deep down, they know it wasn't good. What do you desire for them at that moment? To keep it holed up, unable to tell anyone, sitting in shame? No, you desire for them to confess it to you so that you can help them sort through the big feelings. You want to walk through what they can do differently next time and explain we all make mistakes sometimes. And you long to hug them, assuring them that nothing they can ever do will make you stop loving them. That's what God desires for us as well. He is our Father, and He longs to love us.

Trust, faith, and grace must align to become action. Make a list of things that you will choose to believe. Not with your heart only during church, but every minute of every day.

What do you struggle with? I want you to sit down this week and also physically write down the lies you are believing about yourself. Note the places you feel you are not enough, unworthy, forgotten, unseen, or too far gone, and write out the actual lie. Why is this step important? Because the lies you are believing and have probably believed for a long time are physically affecting your life. So, it is crucial to see them physically written down. Something amazing happens when we do this. We bring it to conscious thought; we can take them captive. You can't take captive what you don't even know exists.

Remember the kindness and grace you showed to a mom you didn't even know? Let's take the first step of practicing grace right now. Knowing what we know, I want you to write either the reasons or the areas you struggle with grace down on paper. Underneath each reason, provide the truth of God's Scripture. Then, put this somewhere you will see it often. Endeavor to cling to these truths over and over and over again. I'll give you one to start:

> There is therefore now no condemnation for those who are in Christ Jesus. For the law of the Spirit of life has set you free in Christ Jesus from the law of sin and death. (Rom. 8:1–2)

9

Compassion

It took roughly five years from beginning this book to getting it on shelves. About a year into writing this book, I went to counseling for the first time in my life. I've never been against counseling—it was my plan to become a counselor at some point—I'd just never been to one. I'd always kind of wanted to, but before then, I had never felt a specific reason to go. I finally scheduled an appointment.

Yet I struggled with hypocrisy. Here, I was writing a book to other moms about perspective, worth, and the way we view motherhood, and I was in counseling—for motherhood. I wrestled hard against these emotions. But the truth is, I knew I needed someone else's objective perspective. I needed some wisdom outside of my own and to have someone look into my life and point things out to me that perhaps no one else could.

In counseling, I recalled a previous season when I was pregnant with Finn, our youngest. I was tired, stressed, chasing two toddlers, afraid of the transition to come, and just in a rough parenting patch. I remember one afternoon in particular was harder, and I felt lower than ever. While I won't disclose all the details of my prayers that day, I couldn't understand why God didn't give my kids a better mom than myself. In my heart, I believed they deserved better, and I wanted that for them more than I wanted the perfect mom label for me. It was a dark place.

> **When I told my counselor my emotions, she told me the word she felt like she was hearing was "shame."**

That season was hard, and life felt like an uphill battle every day, but it had little to do with the particulars and everything to do with what it brought out of me. When I told my counselor about that season, she told me the word she felt like she was hearing was "shame." It's so clear now, but at the time, I just nodded faintly but remained unsure as I listened to her expound on what she meant. She continued to explain that she felt I was dealing with the shame of not measuring up as a mom. It definitely seemed applicable, but *shame*? That word sounded like I'd done something unforgivable and didn't know how to make it right. Other than losing my patience, nothing unforgivable had happened between me and my children. Could shame be what I was feeling? And if it was, what would I do with that?

IT'S NOT SHAMEFUL TO STRUGGLE

The more I thought about it, the more I realized my counselor was right. When motherhood is hard, when we get less sleep, when a transition is brutal, when we receive a diagnosis, when illness strikes, or when trials come our way, those things make life undeniably harder. It can be even more challenging when we feel disappointment in ourselves as we fail to pour out perfection in the face of it. When things get hard, and I want to run away, cry, or throw the towel in, I feel ashamed at feeling that way. I feel ashamed for wishing things were better. Then, after those thoughts surface, I'm tempted to admonish myself for not being more grateful for my situation than I am. After all, there are always things to be grateful for when I'm not so focused on the bad.

I've heard the same sentiments echoed in other moms' words. Moms who are relearning to parent under a new understanding of autism. Moms whose children battle all the ups and downs of an autoimmune disease. Moms who are doing much of parenting alone—or all of it alone—and feeling the weight of the world on their shoulders. There are so many scenarios of different moms where we need a quiet moment to cry out with longing for hardships to be removed and children to be healed or even for them to be obedient or simply sleep. While, yes, I appreciate the perspective shift when we realize things could be worse, sometimes the more we convince ourselves of this, the more we inwardly berate ourselves for ever struggling at all—and so we feel shame.

In another conversation, I confessed to my counselor how I often feel as if I'm not as nurturing as other moms and how this sometimes affects how I feel like I don't measure up. After listening to me, she asked, "When you are caring for your children's needs and taking care of them, do you do it out of love?" I responded affirmatively, "Well, I mean . . . yes, of course, I do love them and make nearly all decisions out of that, no matter what I feel in the moment or not." She pointed out that those actions are nurturing even if I don't *feel* nurturing.

Thinking back over our conversation in its entirety, I realized I do feel shame over how I *feel* while giving no thought or credit to what I *do*. Like the fact that while there have been times I've wanted to run screaming out the front door, leaving only the retreating image of the back of my head, I have refrained. Or the fact that I've wanted to, at moments, leave in the night and call from a distant remote island using an untraceable phone, but instead have woken at 5:15 a.m. like every other morning to get ready, dress my kids, and feed all the mouths once more. What about all the credit I deserve for those things? I'm joking—sort of. But seriously, even though I may want to mentally or physically check out, I remain. And that faithfulness counts for something. Even though I don't know if I can handle the stress and fear any longer, I prevail by taking the hand of God and advocating for my kids once more.

My counselor told me the word I was lacking was self-compassion. "Have you ever heard that term before?" she asked. I had not. Self-love, sure. Self-care, yep. Self-deprecating, I am the queen. But no, not self-compassion. It seemed self-explanatory, I suppose. To have compassion for oneself. But then I thought . . . does it? What does that look like? What exactly is compassion now that I think of it?

If you don't know this about me, I love a good definition. So naturally, I looked it up. According to the *Merriam-Webster Dictionary*, compassion is "the sympathetic consciousness of others' distress together with a desire to alleviate it."* By definition, the only way to have true compassion for someone's circumstances is first to acknowledge they are misfortunate or distressing. It's taking the time to look upon another's situation and consciously say, "That's hard." It leads to a desire for change or that person's deliverance from their current hardship. By this definition, we cannot be

* *Merriam-Webster Dictionary*, s.v. "compassion (noun)," accessed April 30, 2024, https://www.merriam-webster.com/dictionary/compassion.

self-compassionate without first being able to say, "This. Is. Hard." When we don't allow ourselves to say this because we equate it with being ungrateful or unloving, we're not allowing compassion into our own lives. It isn't that we find the compassion we need in or from ourselves—it's that we allow the compassion of Christ to cover our troubles as we would someone else's.

Grace is needed when we *fail.* But compassion is needed when we *feel.*

Though shame can be connected to our actions, I've found it can also be connected to our feelings and thoughts. When I sin, I need grace to cover it. But when we've simply felt some emotion that we don't think a good mom should—when we've felt anything other than absolute gratitude and joy—we don't know where to take that, so we feel shame. Here's what I've learned: Grace is needed when we *fail*. But compassion is needed when we *feel.* We know in order to empathize with others, we have to put ourselves in their shoes. When we do that, we know that their feelings are not failures. Why is it that the last place we are inclined to put ourselves is in our own shoes? Why do we feel like we're failing when we grieve circumstances?

My intelligent, hilarious, and wise friend Emily—who happens to have her PhD in marriage and family counseling—always tells me that two things can be true at one time. We must grasp the realization that we can remain thankful for the good *and* say circumstances are hard at the same time. It's not an either/or game, as the enemy wants us to believe. It's both/and. Maybe what makes all hardships of motherhood exponentially harder is our deep sense of shame in ourselves when we again feel broken by them. Our resistance to such keeps us further from self-compassion.

It may look something like this:

1. I know I need to be grateful for my children, and I am!
2. I know so many have it much worse than I do.

These are true. But we can't allow these truths to discount the fact that we're doing hard things every day, and sometimes they may break us. When a mom cries out in the dark and wishes things could be better, she isn't forsaking her children or even her job. She's longing for ultimate healing from this world. Behind the declaration of "this is hard" is a human heart longing to be not just fully redeemed but also fully healed. And not only is this notion okay—it's necessary.

HURTING IS NOT UNHOLY

We spoke in the last chapter about remembering God's truth constantly and bringing His grace and truth back into the forefront of our minds daily, minute by minute, if we need to. But if we jump straight to Christian platitudes with our feelings and emotions, this is actually avoiding. On the surface, it looks holy and sanctified, but holiness and sanctification come only through the Spirit of the living God. Trying to be so strong that we never feel the pain of hardship is us still trying to be in control. Sometimes surrendering is confession over what we need or have done wrong, but sometimes surrendering just looks like sobbing.

When my sixth-grade teacher called roll, we didn't respond with the classic and boring "Here." Instead, we were required to recite a Bible verse (that, yep, we absolutely memorized the moment we walked into the classroom). For those of you familiar with John

11:35, we were only allowed to use this once. For those less familiar with this passage, it is the shortest verse in the Bible, and it reads, "Jesus wept." While it was the shortest and our favorite for that very reason, it actually says a lot more than we realize.

The fact that Jesus—who was still fully God, though now also fully man—was *weeping* should make us pause. Weeping is not tears in someone's eyes. Weeping is not crying, even. Weeping is when your body wracks with sobs. It's deep with emotion. There's a lot here. Our first question is: What could make the God of the universe weep? The answer is found earlier in verse 33: "When Jesus saw her weeping, and the Jews who had come with her also weeping, he was deeply moved in his spirit and greatly troubled."

If Jesus wept, there is no such thing as becoming so holy we no longer hurt.

Jesus' close friend Lazarus had died, and Jesus arrived at the tomb with Lazarus' sisters, Mary and Martha. The women wept as those who had lost a brother with no hope for his return. Jesus was about to raise Lazarus from the grave, but they did not know this. Jesus knew, yet we still see Him weep. I am not able to unpack all that is transpiring here. I could not begin to understand the mind of God and His thoughts. But there is something that I do understand from this passage. If Jesus wept, there is no such thing as becoming so holy we no longer hurt. If the unblemished Lamb of God sobbed over His friends' grief, then there's no such thing as becoming so sanctified we no longer feel the depths of what is hard in this world. If it didn't make Jesus lesser to weep over the brokenness in this world, then it doesn't mean that for moms.

In Revelation, John wrote:

> He will wipe away every tear from their eyes, and death shall be no more, neither shall there be mourning, nor crying, nor pain anymore, for the former things have passed away. (Rev. 21:4)

As Christians, we use the phrase "we live in a fallen world" all the time. But if we honestly believe this in our hearts, why do we constantly expect an outpouring of perfection from ourselves? Yes, we do know that joy is coming and that He is holding all things. We know eventually all tears will be wiped away and that the pain we experience here will be no more. Eventually, there will be no more crying—we believe this to be true! Yet, we are not there yet. We are here. And when Jesus was here, He wept, too. If Jesus still wept, knowing that He was about to restore what Mary and Martha had lost, then we can weep as we long for the restoration of the brokenness on this earth.

IT'S NOT SINFUL TO HAVE A TROUBLED SOUL

In the book of James, we read:

> Dear brothers and sisters, when troubles of any kind come your way, consider it an opportunity for great joy. For you know that when your faith is tested, your endurance has a chance to grow. So let it grow, for when your endurance is fully developed, you will be perfect and complete, needing nothing. (James 1:2–4 NLT)

While these verses bring us hope that even the darkest moments can be redeemed, sometimes, it feels impossible to find joy in the face of trials. What we need to notice is that these verses don't say we will always *feel* joy; they say we can consider troubles an *opportunity* for great joy. The decisions we make in trials—where we turn, what we do, who we cling to—are all paving paths and creating opportunities that lead us somewhere. Will the decisions we're making in our trials make way for joy later? Are we putting up walls of self-preservation or are we choosing to trust Him another day? Are we clinging to the Lord despite pain, or are we numbing, withdrawing, and distracting? Self-compassion does not mean self-preservation, and it definitely does not mean self-help. Quite the contrary. When we protect "self," we do not hand things over to God. When we acknowledge hardship through self-compassion, we realize our need for God to sustain us.

As mothers, we often move through life expecting ourselves to already be perfect and complete. So, not only do we expect nothing less than to consider trials joy, but there's also this deep disappointment that we would feel opposition to or anything less than joy in such hardships. But really think about this passage. In order to count anything as joy, one has to first *see* their situation as troubling. Faith cannot be tested until it is first called into question. When we feel like breaking or giving up, this is a test. Feeling the temptation is not our final verdict. What matters is what we do despite feeling it. We have to stop letting the wavering in our hearts discount the obedience that follows. If being tested is how we get stronger, why do we insist on despising our initial weakness? It's the starting point of something beautiful. Perhaps the reason we resist acknowledging the depth of the hardship is the prevention from falling apart. Perhaps, however, our falling apart is what God requires.

The flip side is we know that our endurance will never be fully developed here. On this side of heaven, we will never be perfect, complete, or fully healed. We need to heed the call of these verses by realizing that hard circumstances are not the absence of favor in our lives but the evidence of a Father who is taking the time to refine us (and a parent who loves us too much to leave us as we are). In this sense, we can count it as joy when we land in hardship, but we can't and won't ever get to a place where we become so grateful for it that a part of us won't long to escape it. We shouldn't lose this sense of aching for better circumstances or expect to get there because to be fully developed, perfect, complete, and needing nothing is to be in the very presence of God in the kingdom of heaven.

There's this prayer in John 12 that I love. It's Jesus praying to God the Father, and I love the clear picture of Jesus humbly proclaiming what He's feeling and boldly proclaiming what He will do. It occurs when He knows the time is upon Him for the Son of Man to be glorified. The time has come for Him to die. He knows the redemption it will bring for His groaning creation. He knows the salvation and freedom it will bring His people forevermore. He knows the glory it will give to the Father. Yet, He does not skip straight to what is good and necessary without honestly acknowledging what He feels in the moment. It reads, "Now is my soul troubled. And what shall I say? 'Father, save me from this hour?' But for this purpose, I have come to this hour. Father, glorify your name" (John 12:27–28).

With all that Jesus knew and all that He had experienced to get to this very purpose for which He came, He is still honest about what His flesh feels and desires. He admits how troubled His soul is. He even allows us a glimpse into what is tempting—the desire to be removed from this. What Jesus felt did not get the final say. He was obedient to the end for our sake and the glory of His Father.

But I don't want to miss that it was not sinful nor shameful that He said what He did prior to His obedience. In fact, it makes His sacrifice all the more beautiful and deeply moving.

If patience and love were entirely free of endurance and hardship, would they still be kind? If there was no sacrifice to love, could it still be forbearing? For patience to exist, there must first be struggle. For love to be sacrificial, it must first be heavy. We want to always rely on God. We want to be faithful mothers through whatever comes our way. We want to bestow patience and kindness and faith to our children. And we will fail sometimes. But let's not allow the fact that we have an insider's look at our own thoughts and temptations to discount our efforts to keep turning back to what is right over and over.

> **A mom who cries for feeling overwhelmed by what she's facing doesn't have less faith or foresight. She's just feeling the weight of humanity.**

If it were even possible for my weak flesh to embrace hardship fully, it would mean feeling totally at home on earth. But that isn't God's desire for us because this isn't our home. And God doesn't expect this of us—even in matters of our children. A mother who grieves an unforeseen diagnosis for her child does not love her child less or wish her child were "more," but she is a mother who wishes to remove hurts from her child in the struggles her child will face. A mother waking in the night with sick children isn't ungrateful that she has children to wake with—she's just longing for good things, such as sleep for her and her child. A mom who cries for feeling overwhelmed by what she's facing—whether it's a season or a moment—doesn't have less faith or foresight; she's just feeling the weight of humanity. And that's okay, because Jesus felt that, too.

COMPASSION ISN'T COMPETITIVE

Here are some truths on compassion for you. Our hardships don't have to be competitive. We don't have to set them alongside someone else's to see if we have the right to cry or feel broken about our circumstances. We don't have to win the trophy for the "greatest reason to suffer" in order to be struggling. Someone else's trial can be far larger than ours, and it's still okay for us to struggle. We need not justify our hurts before God, who knows our hearts, nor do we need to set a suffering record in order to receive comfort from the Lord. We need only draw near and be honest. Our trials aren't on trial, and He is our ever-ready help in times of trouble.

Our hardships don't have to be competitive. We don't have to compare them to someone else's to determine if we have the right to cry or feel broken about our circumstances.

By longing for ultimate healing from the hardships of this world and the removal of struggle, we can find an even deeper sense of gratefulness that because of Jesus, one day, this dream *will* come to fruition. There are always things, no matter how tough the season, that we can be grateful for in this world. But to never allow ourselves to acknowledge what is truly hard in our lives is to miss the opportunity to be grateful for what is to come. If everything looked great here, why would my eyes ever lift to heaven? If everything in our lives was perfect, why would we need to cry out to God?

Start today by asking: What am I trying to paste on a smile about? What in my life is just really hard right now? If I were looking in as an outsider, what sort of compassion would I have for myself?

As we imitate Christ, we must take that gift of compassion and bestow it on others—for trials, big and small. We also should communicate that those in our lives don't have to justify their hurts to us in order for us to bestow compassion on them. Simply because they know this season won't last and that ultimate healing is coming one day doesn't mean they aren't allowed to be honest about the hardship of trials right now. There is no better gift than having someone you love look at your situation and acknowledge it really is hard and that it's okay to struggle because struggling indicates someone who is fighting and not just giving in. As we do this for others, including our families, let's allow the same to be true for ourselves. When we stop and are honest about what is hard right now, today, God's compassion, which we see so clearly in Jesus, will be there to cover us.

As I think back on myself as a young mom of three tiny people beginning a book on motherhood, I have so much compassion for her. That mom had no idea how much she would need! Writing is hard. Motherhood is hard. Writing *on* motherhood is hard. But Christ's compassion and the Spirit's prompting are what led me every step of the way. The process certainly wasn't always easy, and there were definitely moments of tears, but it's brought so much joy. In fact, it brought you and me this very chapter.

10

Momming like Martha

When I'm asked the question, "What is a good mom?" my first thoughts incline towards the traits and gifts I've seen displayed in good moms I've known. I look at my mother-in-law and how she bakes sourdough for her loved ones and serves and takes care of her chickens. (Seriously, right now, somewhere in the world, my mother-in-law is nursing a chicken back to health as you read this.) I look at my friends who are "put together" or patient or have the best communication tips with their children. I often define what is a good mom by what she does—and often in comparison, what I don't do. And if that's the case, if that's truly what we base being a good mom on, then I've got to lean on my strengths like never before. I better stay on top of what I can do best and where my strengths shine, so that I can be a good mom all of the time. Maybe you do the same thing, and maybe this is why we're so exhausted.

My mom is so organized. She's always on time, has a keen eye for details, and is quick to listen. (Right now, as you read this, she is listening patiently as I verbally process something to death.) I know that she sacrificed so much for me and my siblings that I didn't even see. My mom has more strengths than I could name here. She was and still is a wonderful mom. However, she's confessed to me a few times that she sometimes wonders if this was true. And while I could put a thousand examples of how she is a good mom—including dropping off chicken salad today so I could keep writing—if forced to name the one thing that makes her one, I would have to say it is simply her presence.

I think we often don't see things that way when it comes to ourselves. We question so much if we have anything to offer in and of ourselves that we are addicted to *doing* rather than simply *being*. If I do enough and make enough and serve enough, I will be a good mom, right? If I put forth my best effort and take notes from every good mom I see, I'll arrive. There's nothing wrong with loving our families in physical ways, as we've discussed much in this book. However, I think that when we cannot rest and simply be with our families—when our strivings never cease—there's something underneath those habits that we need to address.

EVERYONE HAS A STORY

I have a podcast. Have I told you that? It's called *The Saltworks*, and the premise is that the word *saltworks* is a literal place where salt is refined. Jesus calls us to be the salt of the earth, which means we can relate to this idea. We are all walking in our callings and being refined day by day. The more figurative meaning of saltworks is slang for jobs viewed as drudgery or mundane. So, the concept is that as we are being refined and sanctified inch by inch while walking in our separate, ordinary corners of the world with the same extraordinary God. Often, much of the refining will happen in unseen places.

With the podcast, I wanted a platform where we could hear each other's stories and bring some of those unseen moments to light. I desired for this to be a place where we could listen to real stories from real people in the real world that we may not otherwise ever get a chance to hear. It's a way to spur on the church to keep going as we each run the race set before us and remember we're not alone.

It's not about the stories. It's about who a person is because of who their God is.

Because of this, people tend to forward me stories. Please hear me say: I love that people who are listening, taking an interest in what I feel passionate about, and are committed to this calling the Lord's given me are reaching out. It's just that sometimes I run across people who are sort of missing the point. Sometimes, people will send me a story or want me to cover one that may not have any faith-based message simply because it is a good story. I love the stories—I do. They are each representative of what the Lord can do when we just walk with Him. But it's not really about the stories. It's about who that person is because of who their God is.

Most often, I see this misunderstanding that it's only about the story when I ask someone if they would be willing to be on an episode, and they hit me with the most used phrase we hear at *The Saltworks*: "I don't really have a story." What they don't realize is that I don't need them to share a news-breaking tale or a gripping story with twists and turns. I just see someone with a certain presence I want to share with the world. Someone whose presence testifies that they are a man or woman who walks closely with the Lord. Someone whose presence tells a story that they've trusted God despite doubts, followed Him despite fear, and seen His goodness despite hardships. Someone whose presence brings with them His presence.

And you know what? I don't fault people one single bit when it's their first inclination to question whether they have a story. Honestly, it's been mine too. *What do I have to share? What do I have to say? Do I have anything of value to bring to the table?* Once again, we come back to the following: we are tempted to measure things by what we can do and not necessarily by who we are by the grace of God.

One woman in the Bible with whom I can relate immensely is Martha. Oh, if I could have Martha on the podcast! If we have podcasts in heaven, I am going to ask her. Because I have a whole lot of questions for her, and I dearly wish we could have her side of the story—especially looking back in hindsight.

MARTHA'S STORY

If you don't know Martha, she and her sister Mary were the sisters of Lazarus, and we discussed them in the last chapter. They were friends of Jesus, and they were the very sisters that Jesus wept with. In today's story, however, we're backtracking to a time when they don't yet know Him. And what do striving women do when they're meeting someone new? Well, they strive, naturally. They strive like somebody's watching.

This particular story is recorded in the Bible in Luke 10:38–42. Here's the rundown: Jesus and His disciples were traveling and came to the village where Martha and Mary lived. While there, Jesus and the disciples went to Mary and Martha's home. Mary is found sitting at Jesus' feet during the visit, but Martha is "distracted by much serving" (Luke 10:40).

The first indication of Martha's inner struggle is the word *distracted*. She wasn't just going through the motions to prepare the dinner (because someone *did* have to make it)—she was *distracted* by it.

Stop right there. Answer me honestly, when someone who has never been to your house is coming to your home, what do you do? They are going to be there for dinner and stay for hours, maybe even for the night. For starters, it's your house, so you're locked and loaded on the hospitality, right? I mean the sheets need to be washed, the floors need to be vacuumed, activities need to be planned, and don't even get me started on the food.

Martha is *there*. She's at hospitality level ten—and she's getting frustrated that Mary is not helping her. I have always wanted to come to her aid and say, "Someone has to cook dinner if you want to eat!" I know, I know! Some of you are going to argue the point that with Jesus, things always turn out. That's true, but we must still do our work.

The first indication of Martha's inner struggle is the word *distracted*. She wasn't just going through the motions to prepare the dinner (because someone *did* have to make it)—she was *distracted* by it. Knowing Martha, it probably wasn't the easiest recipe she had on hand. This was her showstopper. Martha was basically the first Baptist. We like our potluck, and we take it seriously.

I have gone to the same church now for over thirty years. I've seen it grow and morph and accommodate newer times and new faces—and grown it has. In my hometown, the church is large and is able to orchestrate many healthy ministries. Our staff is wonderful and hardworking, and overall, they are willing to shift and change hats as needed. But there is one woman inside our church who holds all the hats, and she does so quietly. She's the person you want to contact if you need something printed, looked up, or located anywhere inside the church walls. She can help you plan an event and find where a staff member is. You name it, she's your girl. Maybe other than the pastor, she is the eyes and ears of the church.

Her name is Sharon Moore. If you've eaten a meal at our church, you've tasted the fruit of her labor. If you've planned, helped with, or attended an event, know that she was somewhere in the background helping orchestrate the details and providing the coordinators with what they needed. Had a baby shower? You guessed it. Sharon Moore. She is on staff, but she is so much more. I wouldn't even know how to give an accurate job description because she just serves in whatever capacity she can—on and off the clock. Every church has a Sharon Moore—the keeper of the keys and servant behind the scenes who knows what needs to be done.

Martha was her village's Sharon Moore. In the Bible, she's recorded to be serving a meal in her house and then later in another's home. This was most likely her job, her life's work, her *identity*. She had it down to a science: timing casseroles and delegating tasks (but maybe not too much delegation because she could probably do it faster than she could give someone else directions). But this night was different. This particular night, she was frazzled over her work, concerned about her guests, and irked by a lack of help during her great time of need. After some time of running around between the various dishes and extra measures she was taking to make this night perfect, she'd had it. She went into the living room.

Maybe she went in there trying to swallow her agitation. Maybe she kept giving Mary the benefit of the doubt as she completed each task and thought her sister would be back to help any minute. After all, Mary knew Martha and how important this was to her. But the time had dragged on, and still, no sign of Mary. Maybe Martha had already chided herself for being impatient and even took a deep breath in preparation to pepper her words with more gentleness. But that was before Martha saw her.

Mary wasn't held back by some other hospitable task. Or caught in a conversation she couldn't escape. Or serving in some other capacity. She was just sitting on the floor! That did it for Martha. This is where we begin to realize that she holds Jesus in high esteem because her question was directed at Him to be the mediator between her sister and herself. She says, "Lord, doesn't it seem unfair to you that my sister just sits here while I do all the work? Tell her to come and help me" (Luke 10:40 NLT).

These women are representing two personalities and two choices. Yet, when we see ourselves and our tendencies in Martha, we can take those verses personally.

Well. *This* has always sounded like a deep-rooted issue to me. It just doesn't sound like this is the very first time Mary has been enraptured by something other than the chores at hand or perhaps unaware of just how much work and attention to detail goes into making a hospitable evening. It sounds like Martha is hoping that surely Jesus will provide justice to a situation that has always bothered Martha.

> But the Lord answered her, "Martha, Martha, you are anxious and troubled about many things, but one thing is necessary. Mary has chosen the good portion, which will not be taken away from her." (Luke 10:41–42)

We tend to oversimplify this story by viewing this as a Mary versus Martha situation. Which was better? Who was right? Whose side did Jesus take? We think it's one personality pitted against another. But this is not an issue of sides. These women are, yes, representing two personalities, but they're also representing two choices. Yet, when we see ourselves and our tendencies in Martha, we take those verses personally.

My first inclination in the past was to be frustrated at the injustice! Finally, she can be justified in her stance and all the hard work she's labored at by herself! Jesus is right there in her living room witnessing the injustice at hand. Yet instead of speaking up for her, He sides with Mary. And when I read that, I feel as if He doesn't side with me. As if I have received the blow myself. As if Jesus has confirmed what I've known all along—that I'm not enough because I'm not a Mary.

THE POWER OF PRESENCE

Recently, I posted a question on social media about what moms want to hear from other moms. One emphatic response was the affirmation encased in the words, "You're a good mom." We want people to see us, even the ugly, and say we're okay. That we're doing our best, and even with the shortcomings, we are *good*. I want to hear that from more than just fellow moms. I want to hear it from my kids. I want to hear it from my parents. I want to hear it from my in-laws. I want to hear it from my husband. But there is *no one* I desire to hear it from more than Jesus. And when I read those words spoken to Martha, I feel like He's shaking His head instead. It is as if, by not supporting Martha's plea to affirm she is right in this situation, He does not reinforce who she is and, by extension, who I am.

I've wrestled with this because I know Jesus, and while this narrative sounds like my insecurities and fears, it does not really sound like Him. Jesus' response does not appear to deliver Martha from the seeming injustice, but this also isn't a story of Jesus admonishing Martha. He corrects her because she has clearly made the wrong decision that night. But remember, Jesus had a goal in all He did: deliverance. He came so that we can have life and have it in abundance (John 10:10). He always speaks truth in love. Knowing this about Him begins to shift the way we read this. If that remains His goal, even here in this story, then He was aiming to deliver Martha. He was calling her into abundant life. He was speaking truth because He loved her.

You see, Jesus didn't just happen into their living room. He was invited, and not by Mary. Verse 38, at the beginning of the story, tells us that when they came into the village, "a woman named Martha welcomed him into her house" (Luke 10:38 NLT). You know what I think? I don't think Martha was distracted in the kitchen because she was missing the importance of who was in her home. I think she was working hard and fretting over the details because she knew to some extent the importance of who was sitting in her living room. For someone who had built her identity such as it was, this was no opportunity to fail. This was no time to sit. Everything had to be perfect for Jesus. *She* had to be perfect.

When I reread His words in this light, everything shifts. First, He addresses her need to feel seen and her need for identity. His address gives me chill bumps: "Martha, Martha," or "My dear Martha" (Luke 10:41 NLT), because these words contain a whole host of affirmations. I imagine He says it with a smile and kind eyes as He stops to show her that He's seeing to her core. Although she's just met Him, His address to her conveys the familiarity of someone who deeply knows her. Like an old friend. Someone who has seen her at every turn and can only smile even at her antics. Automatically, she is known. Maybe Martha was frazzled about having a renowned rabbi in her home, but little did she know she was being addressed by the One who knew her best.

Second, He addresses her inner turmoil: "You are anxious and troubled about many things" (Luke 10:41). In this, I hear acknowledgment of her life's works and service. As if He's seeing more than just what she's doing right now into the labor she's achieved all these years and worked just to hear the words, "You are good." He's not dismissing any of it as trivial. He's saying, "I see the way you've obsessed over even the tiniest things. I see it *all*. Even those things no one else has seen or noticed, I have. None of what you do or what matters to you escapes me." He has seen every single thing she's holding onto.

She is seen. She is loved. She is affirmed. Now, He shifts her focus in love. "There is only one thing worth being concerned about" (Luke 10:42 NLT). He isn't saying that everything she's done isn't appreciated or useful—as we've discussed, Jesus Himself served others. He's telling her that all of her striving is unnecessary when it comes to her value. None of it will make or break her identity and worth or ever make her "good enough."

Jesus' words to Martha were not a dressing-down of her character; they were permission to leave her striving and simply *be*. Jesus wasn't asking Martha to be someone she was not—to be Mary. He was saying Mary's choice of allowing herself to just be present without anything she could do was all that was necessary. He wasn't telling Martha to cease being Martha. His correction wasn't a rejection. He was asking her to come just as she was. That what He valued most about her wasn't her work or her accomplishments, but simply herself. That her presence was good enough for Him.

Jesus' words to Martha were not a dressing-down of her character; they were permission to leave her striving and simply *be*.

THE GOOD PORTION

I'm like Martha. In so many ways, I'm a Martha mom. I know the weight of inviting Jesus in. I know the importance of teaching my children to be like Him and welcoming them just as He would. But often, I desire to feel accomplished and check all the boxes before I sit and give them my full attention because I believe the lies: Having a clean Pinterest home makes me a good mom. Home-cooked meals make me a good mom. Crafts and the neatest new activities make me a good mom. The sweetest books before bed, holiday-themed treats, and attending all the local parades make me a good mom. All of these things are fine and great—they just aren't the good portion.

Hospitality is such a vital part of motherhood. We just don't realize how simply being present is a vital part of hospitality. Just like Martha, understanding who we are is imperative to being able to serve. If we continue to believe we don't mean much to the people around us outside of what we can do for them, we'll continue toiling, trying to earn their approval and we'll miss a greater opportunity. If Jesus could sit in your living room, He'd tell you the same thing: "You are anxious and troubled about many things, but one thing is necessary" (John 10:41–42).

We aren't called to be better, become more, or even be different. We're just called to surrender our striving and be present. Whatever nature God has given us, we bend it to His will in every situation and in every season. Just like Jesus saw all of Martha's labor and worries, He sees ours, too. When we make our one concern sitting at the feet of Jesus, the rest falls into place.

The key to becoming a mom surrendered to the One who never fails is fully discovering that He bears the weight while we need only bear His name. Not only can I come just as I am to be in His presence—but I also can cease trying to become a good mom and simply be present with those who call me mom. They likely won't remember the meals I cooked, how clean the house was, or the crafts we did, but they'll remember how I made them feel. They'll remember that I was there.

11

Playing House

When I was a kid, my cousin and I loved to play "house" when we visited Mamaw. I also played teacher, watched *Balto*, and was married to N*SYNC members (okay, okay, I *pretended* to be married), but playing house was my favorite pastime.

Honestly, though, most of the "playing" was about establishing the scene. In fact, pretty much the entirety of the game was stating our ideals: how many kids we had and what their names were, where we lived, what our homes looked like (a.k.a. which corner of the room was ours), and what our occupations were—essentially, what every aspect of our lives looked like. Naturally, I had about seven kids, was happily and easily married to the lead singer of a boy band (which somehow didn't get in the way of family time at all), and to top it off, I had achieved this by the ripe old age of twenty. Obviously realistic, right? Okay, maybe not.

Cue: the present.

I've been recalling these fond memories and what I love most about them. With these memories, I've also pondered one question.

I think from playing house to living house, we've left out the play.

And my question for you and myself is this: Why don't you and I love playing house now?

I know real life is harder than make believe, and yes, to say things are less than ideal in the real world would be a devastating understatement. There are difficult hardships, bigger decisions, and challenging illnesses. Not to mention our disappointments, discontentment, and selfishness that fight against the 24/7 service sometimes required of us as moms. Yet despite all of these obvious reasons, I can't shake the feeling that it's more than that. You know what I've begun to think? From playing house to *living* house, we've left out the play. And I believe some of that is because we're too focused on the difficult realities of life.

What made our play so fun wasn't constantly focusing on our reality—a couch marking the separation between our "houses" and old calculators for phones—but how we *chose* to see the lives we were building and designing in our play. It was our perspective that mattered. The point of playing house was the enjoyment we received. We would shift and change it throughout the game, gain ideas from each other, and dream as we went.

On top of it all, we were wholeheartedly certain of our decisions, because whose eleven-year-old self isn't totally confident to take on the world with seven kids? Yet here we are, just a *teensy* bit over the age of twenty (give or take fifteen years), building our lives, swallowed by the decisions, and wholly forgetting to put enjoyment back into the equation. As though living house is only all about duty, and playing house was only for fun. But what if it could be both?

A TIME FOR EVERYTHING

I do not know who first coined the phrase "survival mode," but I'm willing to bet big money it was a mom. It's certainly become an essential cultural term in the vocabulary of moms everywhere. I know this mode well. I've walked those days, and I'll walk them again. But these survival-mode seasons aren't forever.

Did you ever babysit? I remember specific babysitting jobs where I would watch multiple kids, feed them, get them into bed, and have the house clean with the dishes done before the mom got home. Easy. Oh, and my mood? Chipper! Why is it that when we were seventeen with probably no idea what we were doing, we could do this and not get bogged down, but at this moment and this age, we feel so overwhelmed by the same tasks?

To be fair, there are innumerable reasons. But I think one large factor in this phenomenon for me is that I knew it ended. I knew, whether it was at 8 p.m. or 11 p.m., I would go home. All I had to do was do a good job for today. That subconscious thought freed me to make things fun for the kids and to make the most of that time because it freed me from the pressure of having to think about tomorrow.

But what if I told you that even though your children likely behave differently for you than a babysitter, and yes, it doesn't always feel as freeing to clean your own home or dishes, this too shall pass? Not only does Scripture explicitly state to not worry about tomorrow (Matt. 6:34), but it tells us there is a time for everything:

> For everything there is a season,
> a time for every activity under heaven.

A time to be born and a time to die.
  A time to plant and a time to harvest.
A time to kill and a time to heal.
  A time to tear down and a time to build up.
A time to cry and a time to laugh.
  A time to grieve and a time to dance.
A time to scatter stones and a time to gather stones.
  A time to embrace and a time to turn away.
A time to search and a time to quit searching.
  A time to keep and a time to throw away.
A time to tear and a time to mend.
  A time to be quiet and a time to speak.
A time to love and a time to hate.
  A time for war and a time for peace." (Eccl. 3:1–8 NLT)

Some tasks of motherhood are drudgery by nature. There's nothing fun about croupy coughs and fever. It's both hard and sad paired with extra work and worry. However, I think it's time to admit that perhaps many aspects of our lives *feel* like drudgery only because we've allowed them to be or because we were told they were. Perhaps someone around us labeled all of them as work, and we've accepted that as fact.

Survival mode is real and necessary sometimes, but it has its place, and its place is not *always*.

I do not believe we, as moms, were ever intended to only trudge through duty, but to take the life we have been given and create. We have talked about how we reflect God and how we're made in His image. Just as He has sacrificed so much—even to the point of the cross—we too, will sacrifice. But that isn't the only facet of His character we will reflect. He's a creative God. He has formed beautiful things—just look out your window and at your children! There's evidence all around us that enjoyment was meant to be had. Sometimes my kids and I just marvel at the fact that He gave us taste buds. We have to eat, but did we have to taste? Or is that just the heart of the Father giving us the ability to delight and enjoy? His creativity matters, and just as He did in the beginning, we too can form order out of chaos.

Yes, there is a time to cry, but are we making time to laugh? Yes, there is a time to grieve, but are we also joining in the dancing when that time comes? Yes, survival mode is real and necessary sometimes. But according to this passage, it has its place, and its place is not *always*. Perhaps right now it's time to learn how to play house again.

A TIME TO DREAM

We've already talked about how sometimes we ask ourselves, "What is the point?" I believe this is one of the most devastating questions we can ask as adults. We look at the fun we used to chase and the dreams we used to aspire to, and four simple words prevent us from pursuing any of them.

Before we go any further, it's time to uproot. It's time to come face-to-face with what lies just beneath that question, specifically as it applies to being moms. The lie that has been secretly sown here is that if something doesn't have absolute reason and utmost importance, it must be discarded as unnecessary in the event of motherhood. This is a problem because we are not all-knowing. We do not know where one endeavor will lead us or how it could grow into the fabric of our lives and others around us. This includes joy.

What if some of the ideals still packed away in the boxes of our hearts could still be accessed and applied to our current reality? But that simple question is enough to stop us dead in our tracks, pack those thoughts back into their box, and push that box back into the attic of our eleven-year-old self's heart. But farmers who watch every cloud never plant, and therefore they never harvest (Eccl. 11:4). I don't know about you, but I want to experience the harvest.

Allow me to replace that doubt-inducing question with new ones to ponder: What if the point is to bring enjoyment back into your life as a mother? Do you even think that enjoyment, merriment, and play—not just for your children, but for you—are worth value anymore?

The mother who instills enjoyment and fun into her own life builds magic into the lives of her children. We work so hard to create crafts, memories, and activities for each child, and we should. This intentionality is needed yet often missing in the world. But what if much of what's needed is simply that our children see us coming alongside them and living our lives to the fullest? I have a question for you: What would that even look like for you?

The mother who instills enjoyment and fun into her own life builds magic into the lives of her children.

Take a moment and dream with me. Get a piece of paper or your journal and write at the top "My Mom Ideals." Now, as you make your list, I want you to think of other moms who inspire you, different eras you might love, favorite social media accounts, and hobbies you enjoy or perhaps never-ventured hobbies you would love to learn. I'm going to include my list here so you can have an example. This is brainstorming, so nothing can be wrong or too small or silly to include. Feel free to steal some of mine, but honestly, think about what *your* ideals might be. Not your mom's. Not your friend's. Not the world's. Just yours. They can range from silly to serious, from little to big. Put them all.

Here are some of mine:

- Embrace fashion in my everyday life
- Have some candlelit dinners at night as a family
- Read through chapter books together
- Explore new cities or countries together
- Learn to sew and play tennis
- Continue to teach my children their worth and identity are rooted in Christ
- ~~Become an author~~
- Raise individuals who have varied interests and dreams
- Learn to cook vegetables my children will willingly touch
- Lead small Bible studies with other women
- Exercise more
- ~~Start a podcast~~
- Set regular date nights

This list of mine is not exhaustive. It's not a full brain dump of everything I would like to do or prioritize in my lifetime. But it is a glimpse of what it could look like. The point of the list you've just made is not to create the perfect life or benchmarks you have to meet to find true joy. We know without a doubt the joy of the Lord is our strength. The beauty of this list is that yours doesn't have to look anything like mine and that both of ours can change anytime we'd like it to. So, what is the point?

Let's return to your list. What is on it? Are there wild items that seem entirely impossible? Good. Because that means you allowed yourself to be free and to dream big, and moms are allowed to do that. Take the item that calls out to you the most. Is it missing from your life because it's not *plausible* in this season, or because you've been told things cannot be that way? Is it because you haven't even voiced it to your husband or family because you asked, "What is the point?" and that stopped you? We know without a doubt that our God wants us to know that in Him, nothing is impossible. But I truly believe He also wants us to know that in Him, nothing is too wonderful either. The question is: Do you believe that?

We know without a doubt that our God wants us to know that in Him, nothing is impossible. But I truly believe He also wants us to know that in Him, nothing is too wonderful either.

Take the first item on my list: to embrace fashion in my daily life. I know this seems silly, but it's something I love. Could I live without it if God asked me to? Of course! But has He? Honestly, no. I feel no conviction against wearing what feels fun within the conventions of modesty. I just began to believe that, like all other mom cultures, leggings and T-shirts were required. That this was the only way to be a stay-at-home mom of littles. Now, do not hear me say that your list is anything other than wonderful if yours began with "living in leggings." If it does, DO IT! There are no rules that say you cannot. I only say this to ask: Why is it that moms have simply accepted these unspoken rules that can actually be changed to fit the life you want? But it honestly lifts my spirits and adds fun to my day when I allow myself to play dress-up, even if I'm changing diapers and no one sees me or I'm editing at a coffee shop.

What about those untapped hobbies you've had on the back burner for a solid fifteen years? Is it possible to learn new skills or pursue new interests as a mom? Absolutely, it is! Is there a law against someone over eighteen taking tennis, piano, sewing, or dance lessons? No. Do you have to do schooling, discipling, teaching, living, or cooking like your friend group or family does? No, you don't.

We spend far too much time trying to figure out what we feel we *should* do and not enough asking what we'd *like* to do. We invest far too much effort into conforming to what we think we should be and not near enough to who we want to be, who we just are, and who God created us to be. We waste far too much time asking which decision is the *right* one without asking: Is it truly a matter of righteousness? Most often, the "best" choice has nothing to do with right and wrong and everything to do with preference. And preference does not have to be determined by uniformity—even in motherhood.

A TIME TO ACT

I want to give you another list now. It's not mine—it's actually from the Bible. It's pulled from Proverbs 31, in which we find the description of what many have called "the ideal woman." If you've never read it and would like to read the passage yourself, go ahead. But for time's sake, I'm going to list here not her ideals and dreams but what this passage says she does:

- Spins her own flax and wool
- Gets up before dawn to prepare her household's breakfast
- Plans the servants' work early in the morning

- Inspects a field and buys it with her own earnings
- Uses the profit from the field to plant a vineyard
- Works hard, bringing energy and strength into all she does
- Helps the poor and needy
- Makes sure everyone in her household has warm clothing
- Makes her own bedspreads
- Dresses in fine clothes
- Runs a business by making and selling linen clothes and accessories
- Laughs without fear of the future
- Uses wisdom and kindness in her instructions
- Manages her household well, refusing to give into laziness
- Fears the Lord

Just curious. How do you feel after reading that list? Do you feel exhausted? Overwhelmed? Annoyed? Perhaps you're even rolling your eyes? If you answered yes to any of these, you are not alone. In fact, I'd say you find yourself in the vast majority. But before we get stuck on any one thing, let's talk about her.

Did you know she was also a wife and a mom? This detail is so interesting because we aren't really given much to go on as far as how she mothers. The only reason we know she is one is because we're told in Scripture that her children bless her. I know, I know. What seemed like impossible standards before we realized that now seem doubly so. How in the world are these her accomplishments *and* she has children and a husband that make her feel seen and respected?

But did you also know that she actually wasn't real?

She wasn't. This ideal woman was merely just that—an ideal. She was a sort of poem created by King Lemuel's mother. It was spoken to him in such a way that we might teach children rhymes or songs to remember the life lessons or principles they hold. Like others of this nature, these words were not meant to be the *exact* thing King Lemuel would find in a wife. They were attributes to teach his mind to search for character. She's the product of words crafted by a mother in such a manner that his mind would easily play back and be unable to forget when it came time to find a wife. She's the representation of attributes that, maybe as a whole, might represent a wife whose heart is good and pure.

It's important to understand this because, *of course,* these are impossible standards. Of course, they are not found in one person alone—at the very least, in the same season. And truly, the point was never about any one attribute, even to King Lemuel's mother, but rather the heart reflected in them. But if it's not meant to be a checklist for each one of us on how to be a virtuous woman or mother, what can we take away from it individually?

Look at what we see in this woman. We see someone who doesn't just have an idea occasionally. She has many, and she acts on them. She's turning a profit everywhere she goes—she's an entrepreneur. But she isn't just making wise investments; she's also creative. She creates beautiful things for herself and others. She is a caretaker and nurturer. Everyone in her household—family and servants—is taken care of in their needs. She's organized. She knows what needs to be done and can efficiently delegate who needs to do what and when. She's fashionable. She wears the finest clothes her time has to offer, but doesn't let this stop her from being industrious. She is well-spoken. She is known in all of her operations and words as wise and kind. On paper, this woman is a jack-of-all-trades!

It's an understatement for you and I to read this together and say we can't do all of that or aren't gifted at all of that! Guess

Not only do failures and struggles *inside* motherhood never prevent you from being a good mom. But biblically speaking, neither do your interests and dreams *outside* of motherhood prevent you from being a good mom.

what—no one is! Especially not all in one season. However, there is a benefit in this seemingly all-inclusive list. I bet every single one of us can find one or two aspects that reflect our gifts and skills in this one woman. You may be the most nurturing soul, but owning your own business? No way. Or you may feel totally confident in starting a business and dressing up every day, but organization? No, thanks. Or maybe you adore creativity and can turn anything into treasure, but having to be well-spoken? No, ma'am. I'm trying to make the point that this list—yes, beautiful and wonderful all wrapped up together—was never meant to make you feel like you aren't measuring up as a woman or a mother. But when we stop to find ourselves in her attributes and identify the things we see highlighted that make us come alive, we get to have those very things that are found in us affirmed by the Word of God. And that's pretty cool.

Any one of these endeavors on its own has been deemed worthy and excellent when yielded to the Lord. So, find freedom in that. You're allowed to be a mom and a business owner. You're allowed to forgo ever making a dollar and enjoy simply creating and nurturing, should your situation allow it! You're allowed and should view your gift of organization as spiritual and life-giving to those around you. (I can personally assure you not everyone has that knack.) You're allowed to be well-spoken and wise and still love a good outfit moment.

What I want you to hear in this chapter is that not only do failures and struggles *inside* motherhood never prevent you from being a good mom. But biblically speaking, neither do your interests and dreams *outside* of motherhood prevent you from being a good mom.

The key to this woman is held in the words "the woman who fears the LORD" (Prov. 31:30). This woman feels full of joy. She laughs and chases down worthwhile pursuits, but every step of the way, she fears the Lord. She has reverential awe and a perfectly placed trust in the One who holds everything and makes everything meaningful. She seeks to do nothing outside of His will or His presence.

If you think about it, she's the depiction of the very opposite of what we originally saw in Eve's fall. Even in perfect circumstances, Eve reached outside of God's presence in hopes of gaining more godlike attributes. This woman, though very successful and well-rounded, seeks to do nothing and gain nothing outside of the hand of God. She also doesn't try to do everything in her power, despite what it looks like. Her accomplishments are many and are impressive indeed, but one of her accomplishments is delegating to others what she cannot do on her own.

It makes me wonder. Though we admit wholeheartedly that we cannot do everything on our own, what do we physically change to acknowledge that truth? Do we ask for help? Do we hire anything out? Do we sink into feelings of failure when we can't do it all? Or do we look to God both for fulfillment and for enjoyment?

A TIME TO PLAY

Do you know what your eleven-year-old self knew that your grown-up self has forgotten? That she was allowed to be her. That mistakes were allowed and changes were welcome. That she could try something and switch it back if it didn't work. That she was wonderfully loved and her worth wasn't dependent on perfection or how she compared to everyone else. That she could dream and create a life of wonder even amid the mundane and hard. That she *could* enjoy and was *supposed* to enjoy life. That it wasn't about what the life next to hers looked like. That her own life could hold seeming incongruences. That life wasn't just what happened to her but also what she made it. That she could play.

What your eleven-year-old self *didn't* know that your grown-up self does is that she now has even more freedom because she's alive and firmly rooted in Christ Jesus. No difference, choice, decision, failure, hobby, or outfit is going to make or break her. Only He gets to define her worth and who she is. (And He delighted in designing you. So, you can have fun creating, too.)

The beauty of motherhood is that we are not left to do it alone. Yes, some of the responsibility is still largely ours, but we don't need to miss the joy that will season our lives if we'll only stop to *play* again. Of course, we'll meet our lives with a sense of determination to meet our roles as moms with persistence. But it's just as important to note that in the moments and places we can, it's not selfish nor wasted to play. In fact, it's *good*. So, I want to ask you: If you were playing house right now, what would *you* do?

12

Well Done

One day I was preparing to speak to a group of college students. I planned to talk mainly on the weight and importance of God's Word. I was basically posing the question: Do we turn to His Word again and again, no matter what we face, as if it actually has the power and sustenance to change and renew us in all things? Do we truly believe that? I was working on this when a good friend called me who was currently walking through the unimaginable.

I paused my preparations to visit with her over the phone, and we began to get into what it looks like to abide in the Lord. She posed the question, "I mean . . . I've walked with the Lord a long time. So, this may be a dumb question to ask out loud. But what does it even look like to abide?"

It was one of those conversations that dove in deep, and as we processed what it might look like or feel like, it hit me. I said, "You know what, if we could definitively define that and if I could give these college students a step-by-step process, that would be awesome—but it would sort of not be abiding at all." The truth is that abiding and remaining in the Lord means that we will depend on Him for all things, not gain proficiency and independence enough to leave Him and do it on our own.

I think the question we've been mulling over this entire book is much the same. The truth is, not only can I not give you a step-by-step guide on how to be a good mother, but that would actually be counter to the theology I hold on the subject. You see, the word *good* is such an interesting word. We're asking one of the most universal questions with a word holding the least universal definition: How does anyone define good?

THE VERDICT IS IN

Many things in our lives can easily measure what's good. When I try a new recipe, I know on the first test if it's good or not. If I go out and take a test, there's a grade that tells me if I did well. If I enter a sports competition of sorts, it will be easily apparent if I measure up or not (believe me, this will be the easiest of all—verdict: not good). My point is that in so many other areas, we can assess how good someone is at something because there is a measure or a progress report of kinds. Motherhood is not so because our children cannot be our progress reports.

In so many other areas, we can assess how good someone is at something because there is a measure or a progress report of kinds. Motherhood is not so because our children cannot be our progress reports.

Our children can't be the measure because they are human. They are their own people with their own free will. We'll teach them and they'll defy it. We'll lead them, and they'll veer off. We'll discipline, and they'll do it again. We know this, because we've seen it and we also did this when we were kids. What's more is that they'll age and move out one day and this all-encompassing season of motherhood will be gone. We'll still be moms, but it won't be our trade the way it is now. Our children will grow, make mistakes, forge their own ways, and some may not choose what we've trained them to seek. Some may even walk away from their faith. Here's what I want you to hear: Why should that mean you're not a good mom?

The truth is that we can't measure our worth by any of these means. Only Jesus Christ can determine our value, and we can never let anything mark our lives more than the blood of Jesus. However, I know we still beg to hear the answer to the question, "Am I a good mom?" We want a measuring scale.

Nothing in the Christian faith is ever in the output. It's always in the input—and our input is faithfulness.

The issue with any progress report is they never really take into account how much you've studied or sacrificed. They don't factor in the effort. Like a college exam, you could have studied all your class notes until you knew them frontwards and backwards, only to show up and realize the test is solely from the textbook. At the end of the day, the only thing progress reports can do is measure whether you passed or failed.

But motherhood isn't a test to see if we've passed or failed. We aren't waiting for the results to come in or for the output to determine whether or not we're good enough. We can't live in fear of how things will work out or what our children will choose today or tomorrow as if we're waiting on the jury to come back in and tell us. Not only will this fluctuate every single day based on what we are seeing, but this is also unbiblical. Nothing in the Christian faith is ever in the output. It's always in the input—and our input is faithfulness.

THEY WERE NEVER MINE

In the week leading to His death, Jesus says, "Who then is the faithful and wise servant, whom his master has set over his household, to give them their food at the proper time? Blessed is that servant whom his master will find so doing when he comes" (Matt. 24:45–46). He goes on to describe this in a parable in Matthew 25, and this is the Hallie Dye summary of the story.

A master going away for some time entrusts three servants with various amounts of his property to watch over in his absence. The first, he gives five talents; the second, he gives two talents; and the last, he gives one talent. Now, right off the bat, we note the varying amounts, and Scripture does say that these are given to the servants based on their abilities.

However, what we can easily miss is that one talent alone is worth roughly *twenty years' wages* for a laborer. I don't know for sure what the average income of an American is, but let's consider all jobs and say, for argument's sake, it's fifty thousand dollars. (But you can do your own math for your income to put this into perspective). Taking that number and plugging it into today's economy, that is equivalent to one *million* dollars to the least of these servants. These are no small sums, even if the third servant's is smaller than the others. In comparison, yes, it is less, but at face value, he, too, has been entrusted a large portion. Though the master has much, each of these talents given is precious and worth much.

What's more, these three servants are bond servants. Unlike laborers, they receive no wages—this is their life's work. In other words, they aren't going to get paid any more or less based on what they do with their master's property. What they will do with these amounts will purely be based on their loyalty and faithfulness to the master.

The first servant with five talents (by our measure, five million dollars in today's terms) takes his amount and immediately goes and trades with them and makes five more. The second servant, given two talents, goes and makes two more. The last servant goes and digs a hole, places the amount he was given in there, and leaves it. We could speculate a lot about why he did this here, but we'll wait until we hear the master's response.

When the master does return, much time has gone by. The servants come forth to settle their accounts with the master and report their returns. After each of the first two servants, the master says to each individually, "Well done, good and faithful servant. You have been faithful over little; I will set you over much. Enter the joy of your master" (Matt. 25:21–22). Then, the third servant steps forth and reports what he's done: nothing.

I feel like the atmosphere switches here. Like if we were standing in the room with this master and servants, we've just gone from smiles, laughter, slaps on the back, and cheering to silence. The joviality is gone and an unsteady silence fills the room from which we wish we could all soundlessly slip away without anyone noticing.

He clears his throat. "Master, I knew you to be a hard man, reaping where you did not sow, and gathering where you scattered no seed, so I was afraid, and I went and hid your talent in the ground. Here, you

I don't see *any* of the qualities in the master that this third servant does. And maybe that's kind of the point.

have what is yours" (Matt. 25:24–25).

I have wrestled over these words many times over the years. It's such an odd response to me. We've seen no harsh or hard qualities of the master thus far in the story. He's been abundantly generous, and he's trusted these servants with a lot of responsibility—even given them free rein to make the decisions with what he's entrusted to them. He didn't provide a detailed, high-expectation checklist. He didn't meticulously count the talents when the others stepped forward or say, "Oh, this is all you were able to do?" He trusts, he leaves, he returns, and he encourages and praises the good and faithful servants. I don't see *any* of the qualities in him that this third servant does. And maybe that's kind of the point. Maybe the largest reason this description of the master seems so off base is because this servant doesn't really *know* the master.

I imagine an ominous silence here—thicker than before. Then, the master speaks. "You wicked and slothful servant! You knew that I reap where I have not sown and gather where I scattered no seed?" (Matt. 25:26). (Notice the question form here—in other words, "You *knew* this to be true?") Then he continues, "Then you ought to have invested my money with the bankers, and at my coming I should have received what was my own with interest" (Matt. 25:27). He then gives the talent to the others and pronounces judgment on that servant.

This story is so strange because it feels like there are pieces missing. The master jumps straight to judgment without any more questions. Why? The servant may not have understood the master, but the master perfectly understood the servant.

The master's point was that even if what the servant thought about him was true, he could have taken the talent to a more secure place that gained, at the very least, interest. And why wouldn't the servant have done this?

Well, this will all be speculation, but let's speculate on the words "wicked and slothful" (Matt. 25:26), shall we? Slothful, we know to be lazy. This servant didn't want to do anything more with his talent. The only thing he did was do the work to dig the hole. He put no time or effort into thinking through what he could do with the talent, where it would be best kept, or ask anyone for advice—he just buried it. But why the word *wicked*?

I think this is where the master could see into the servant's heart, just as the Lord can see into ours. That servant, as we mentioned, was a bond servant. He didn't make wages because his life's mission by legality was to be a servant to this master. That means that he didn't necessarily stand to gain anything by his work with the talent. It wasn't his talent, and he wasn't going to receive a bonus, so he didn't care that much about it. His heart was concerned with himself, not the master's good. Perhaps he even felt less inclined to do much with it because he looked upon the five talents in the first servant's hands, the two in the second servant's hands, and didn't think the one talent in his hands was worth his effort. But how can a sum—a treasure—be precious enough to the master who has much and be worth so little to a servant that it becomes buried in the backyard? How can the master look at his servant, entrust him with an item he deems precious, and then have the servant—who has no possessions, money, or purpose outside of his service—deem it not worth his time or notice? Indeed, the words *wicked* and *lazy* start to make more sense.

This servant is undeniably important to look at. We've all been guilty at times of not possessing the eyes of the Lord as we look upon a service or matter that we think is small but that He deems important. How can we be entrusted with a hard or waiting season He's given, our children, the finances that He's deemed enough, the job He's provided, the talents and giftings He grants, and think they aren't worth the time and effort necessary to invest? All of these things were never really mine—they were His to begin with. So, how can I think anything that is His is anything less than precious? Yet, I have. And assuredly, I will again.

So, this servant is a humbling reminder to always remember even when we think we have little in comparison by way of money, influence, purpose, gifts, you name it, we have the amount that we have because of *Him*. It's His; it was never ours. May we never hold with contempt what He entrusted to us with care.

SIMPLY ABIDE

Yes, there's a good and indispensable lesson in that third servant, but I want you to look right now at what you're holding. Yes, literally. A book. And not just any book—a book written to help you ask the Lord if you're a good mom. Not only are you holding it, you're in the last chapter. You've stuck it out and you're in the home stretch, still seeking. Still asking.

So, I want to ask *you* something: Does that seem like something the third servant would do? Does that seem like something an uncaring mom would do?

Before we go on, I think you need to take stock of that for a minute and ask objectively what that says about you as a mother.

Because I know the time it took you to read this, the money it took you to buy it, and the commitment it took you to keep asking despite fearing what you might find.

Yes, you aren't perfect.

Yes, you will have failings—some small and some big.

Yes, your kids will tell you that you've hurt their feelings or let them down.

Yes, you'll have to repent seven hundred times over.

Yes, you'll wish you had done something differently.

Yes, you'll learn better ways after trying a few that don't work.

Yes, your children's choices in life are not guaranteed.

Despite all that isn't good or doesn't *feel* good or doesn't look good—you're still a good mom. A good mom cares. A good mom tries. She invests. She learns. She fails. She gets up and goes again. She apologizes—over and over. She models repentance and obedience. She loves. But above all, a good mom looks to the Lord for each step along the way. Always. The point of being a good mom isn't to gain the title of "Good Mom." It's to abide in Him. Everyday. Every moment. There is no perfect checklist. There are no direct instructions or guarantees of the return our investment will make. There are only the precious gifts entrusted.

The point of being a good mom isn't to gain the title of "Good Mom." It's to abide in Him.

I wanted you to see the third servant, but I also wanted you to see where you are. Will you and I have third-servant moments? You bet. I'm having one today. But if we are in Christ Jesus, you and I *can't* be the third servant because we know Him. We know

His goodness and His character, and we chase after both, or we wouldn't be here, begging for His blessing on our walks of motherhood. If you are a follower of Jesus Christ, you are not the wicked and lazy servant. So, let's revisit the first two.

Remember, the master did not leave instructions. He did not say, "Remember to water the plants. See my steward about the investments. Make sure if you trade, they give you a fair price." He doesn't say any of that. There is no micromanagement in this master. It simply says he "entrusted to them his property. . . . Then he went away" (Matt. 25:14–15). Same thing with his return. He doesn't say, "Well, did you do it that way? Oh, well, I would have set up this kind of fund because that would have gotten you more return." No. He does not nitpick about the way these two servants invested his property. In fact, we don't even know how the second servant made his other two talents. Scripture doesn't say. It isn't even important enough to note. Why? Because it wasn't about the how—it was about the why. It wasn't about being the best, it was about goodness.

Just like the third servant, the first two were also bond servants. They, too, had nothing to gain outside of what the master gave or the amount they earned with it. They took his property, and they did something with it out of sheer loyalty and obedience to the good of the master. Not only does he not get tedious over how they've made these amounts, but the heart of truth is also in his response. Notice what he *doesn't* say here. Because these two servants have taken what they were given and, by the best means they knew how, made more. As we've established, these were no small sums. Yet, the master does not say, "Well done, successful servant." He does not say, "Well done, industrious servant." He does not say, "Well done, effective and efficient servant." He doesn't say that.

Remember what he said? "Well done, good and faithful servant," (Matt. 25:21, 23). Yet, how often are the first three fictitious responses how we measure our efforts in motherhood? And not just in motherhood, but in all matters of faithfulness?

The master calls these servants good because their hearts were for the good of the master. They cared. The master calls these servants faithful because they took their care for him and they *did* something about it. They were obedient. It never mattered about the details—it was always about their hearts. The same is true for us.

We'll always be moms, but the role of mom won't always be the main part of our lives or time. Not only can we not idolize the role of mom because it isn't eternal, but we can't dictate what we think is worth our investment. Whether it's inside motherhood or something else entirely, whatever is placed in front of us, we need only be faithful. The outcome, the output, the success rate—these aren't ours to hold. Neither are these what deem a servant "good." What deems a servant of any kind "good" is her faithfulness.

Maybe what we need to hear even more than "You're still a good mom" is "Well done, good and faithful servant." If we live with that intent and set our sights on Him and all He deems worthy, we can't miss it. He makes all things good, including moms.

Acknowledgments

Any and all glory goes to God. He has carried me through this journey, season of life, and this message. There were so many times I quit, yet He brought refinement in each return to this book. This book would not be here without His grace, truth, and also His providence of how it came to be. I know it was all Him in these pages, because I'm still learning them. Thank you, Father, for leading me to surrender over and over. You have done abundantly more than I could ever ask or imagine.

To my absolute favorite person, Andrew Dye. To say I couldn't have done this without you would be an understatement. You believed in me when I didn't. You saw this book becoming more when I still can't. In all the hours of letting me write, in investing in my writing and *The Saltworks* podcast, in listening to me read aloud (again) in the kitchen while you were cooking, you believed. Thank you for loving the person on and off these pages. Thank you for being the best husband, father, and the one who makes me laugh most. Some of these chapters couldn't have been without the way that you have loved me like Christ. I'm so proud to share your wisdom and grace with the world in this book.

To my children Bear, Garnet, and Finn: for being such gifts that point me toward the Lord whether you realize it or not. You all love so big, and I'm so proud to be your mom.

To my mom, Sharon Evans: Thank you for being such a good mom and now one of my best friends. Thank you for the babysitting and chicken salad that fueled long days of writing or editing. Thank you for showing me what it looks like to seek the Lord at every stage and turn of life. Your strength and wisdom have made me who I am today, and I am so grateful for you. You are, without a doubt, a good the best mom.

Thank you, Lindsay King, for being the phone call where I can dive into deep theological questions, the person I can laugh with, and the one who still makes me dance. Your teaching and way with words have forever impacted my life, and I am so privileged to get to learn from you as you mother your three kids so well. I'm so grateful you're my sister.

To Amy Dye, the best mother-in-law there ever was. Thank you for keeping my kids and loving them so well on days I was crafting this message. Thank you for the endless supply of sourdough and love.

Thank you, Abby (Perkins) Smith for coming religiously in the summertime so I could write furiously! This book wouldn't be without you. Thank you.

Lindsay Stagg, thank you for being there through every stage of this wild roller coaster. From high school dating to parenting, you've been there, and this book was no different. If it weren't for you, I would have had to choose between the podcast or the book, but you stood in that gap, just like you stand in the gap with prayer.

Thank you—not just for being beside me in everything but truly pointing me toward the Lord over and over. I don't know where I'd be without you.

To Emily Jones, for reading probably every chapter as I finished them—before any of us knew what it would be—and coming back with feedback and encouragement. Thank you for being a voice of reason, genuinely one of the funniest humans to ever live, and for your words of affirmation in so many areas. I firmly believe everyone should know Emily Jones.

Thank you, Erica Johnson, for always hearing me and making me feel seen in this process and in motherhood. Thank you for speaking into my doubts and fears in writing and ministry. Thanks for letting me be me.

Heather Smith, thank you for the long days of surviving (and thriving) in motherhood with me. The Finns and the Davids stick together. Thank you for celebrating the milestones of this process when I was still reeling with imposter syndrome and making me laugh constantly. Thanks for being the best neighbor a girl could ask for.

Bethany Wilson, we both know I wouldn't be here without you. You supported me and believed in the book I think before I did. Thank you for pushing me and encouraging me into places I never would have dared. Thank you for being the hands and feet of Jesus not just to myself, but to so many.

Thank you, Tara Fuller and Amy Farris. You've shown up for me more times than I could count. You've encouraged me in ways I'll never forget. Thank you for the texts, the meals, the support, words, and most importantly, the prayers.

To Cheryl White, for being a mentor that took time out of your busy mom life to pour encouragement, hope, and grace into mine. For seeing me when I felt like I could chaotically fly under the radar in the church parking lot. You have brought peace and courage into my life in many moments. I'm so grateful for your mentorship.

Thank you, Trillia Newbell, for meeting this Monroe, Louisiana, girl playing host for a weekend event and thinking she could possibly have something to share with the world. You didn't just give me a chance—you gave me wisdom, encouragement, and direction. I'll never forget you praying over me asking the Lord to guide my hands in every single step of this process. That prayer has become my anthem, and it shaped this entire publishing journey for me. I would never have believed or even tried had you not pushed me and believed in me. This book literally wouldn't exist without you. I have cherished every direction and bit of wisdom you've given me. Thank you, deeply.

Thank you, Ashleigh Slater, my incredible editor with Moody. You so graciously took these disorganized chapters and made it a cohesive book. These words would not be the same without you—literally. You challenged me, heard me, and encouraged me tremendously. It brought me immense peace so many days knowing the manuscript was in your hands and under your wisdom. A girl could not ask for a better editor. Thank you so much.

Thank you, Stephanie Chou. You were the first to comb through a half-baked manuscript from a wannabe author. Would I have even gotten a book deal without your prior coaching and editing? Thank you for making me laugh out loud with your comments and pushing me to be a better writer. (Thank you, Morgan Aitken, for connecting us!)

A special thank you to my first readers and proofreaders for taking the time out of each of your busy schedules to provide feedback. I value each of your opinions so much, both in writing and in life. Sharon Evans, Lindsay King, Jayme Stokes, Lu Ann Butler, Emily Jones, Lindsay Stagg, Erica Johnson, Laura Katzenmeyer, Alyson Owen, Amy Givler, Clara Crossland, and Rebekah Clayton.

Lastly, but certainly not least, to everyone at Moody Publishers for giving me this chance, thank you. You didn't have to take a risk on me, but I will be forever grateful. Every step of the way I felt heard and seen and allowed to ask all the first-time beginners questions without judgment. I thank the Lord for each and every one of you. Thank you, from the bottom of my heart.

The Saltworks

The Saltworks are the stories of real faith from real people in the real world. Saltworks by definition is a place where salt is refined as well as a job often viewed as drudgery. But it's in the unseen places where people just like you are refined to walk faithfully in their everyday lives, because God works in the saltworks. The Bible is full of these people, and they live right next door to you.

They are the salt of the earth. These are their stories, and this is your story.

AVAILABLE WHEREVER YOU LISTEN TO PODCASTS

You finished reading!

Did this book help you in some way? If so, please consider writing an honest review wherever you purchase your books. Your review gets this book into the hands of more readers and helps us continue to create biblically faithful resources.

Moody Publishers books help fund the training of students for ministry around the world.

The **Moody Bible Institute** is one of the most well-known Christian institutions in the world, training thousands of young people to faithfully serve Christ wherever He calls them. And when you buy and read a book from Moody Publishers, you're helping make that vital ministry training possible.

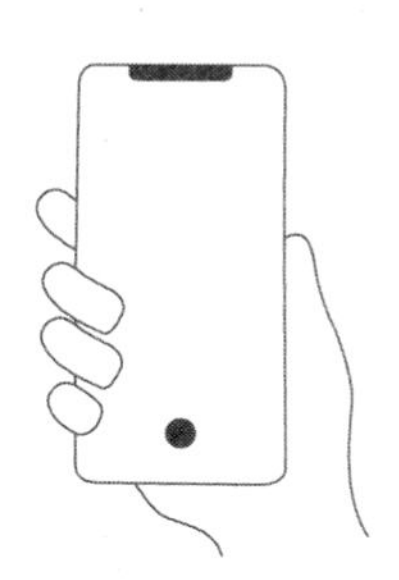

Continue to dive into the Word, *anytime, anywhere.*

Find what you need to take your next step in your walk with Christ: from uplifting music to sound preaching, our programs are designed to help you right when you need it.

Download the **Moody Radio App** and start listening today!